THE TASTE OF OUR TIME

Collection planned and directed by

ALBERT SKIRA

BIOGRAPHICAL AND CRITICAL STUDY

BY

NELLO PONENTE

Translated from the Italian by James Emmons

KLEE

SKIRA

Title page:
Arab Song, 1932. Oil. Phillips Collection, Washington, D.C.

★

Distributed by Crown Publishers, Inc.
419 Park Avenue South, New York, N.Y. 10016

© 1960 by Editions d'Art Albert Skira, Geneva
Library of Congress Catalog Card Number: 60-8729
New edition 1972

Reproductions authorized by Cosmopress, Geneva

CHRONOLOGICAL SURVEY

1879 Born at Münchenbuchsee, near Bern, on December 18th, of a German father and a Swiss mother, both accomplished musicians.

1886-1898 Attends school in Bern.

1893 Building of the Hôtel Tassel in Brussels, designed by Victor Horta.

1895 The magazine "Pan" comes out in Berlin, edited by Bierbaum and Meier-Graefe.

1896 The magazine "Jugend" launched in Munich.
Jawlensky and Kandinsky arrive in Munich from Russia.

1897 Founding of the Vienna Secession by Gustav Klimt.

1897-1898 August Endell designs and builds the Elvira Studio in Munich.

1898 Klee completes his schooling in Bern. Leaves in October for Munich, where he enrolls in Knirr's art school.

1898 First Secession exhibition in Vienna.

1899 Founding of the Berlin Secession, with Max Liebermann as chairman.

1900 Studies at the Munich Academy in Franz Stuck's class.

1900 Kandinsky and Marc study at the Munich Academy.
Founding of the "Phalanx" group in Munich.
Max Beckmann attends the Art School at Weimar.
Antonio Gaudi builds the labyrinth of the Parque Grüell in Barcelona.
Paris World's Fair.

1901 Trip to Italy in October with the Swiss sculptor Hermann Haller.

1901 Kirchner and Bleyl study architecture in Dresden.
Beginning of Picasso's Blue Period.

1902 Kandinsky elected chairman of the Phalanx group in Munich.
Pictures by Munch, Hodler and Kandinsky exhibited at the Berlin Secession.

1903-1904 Series of grotesque etchings. Influenced by Blake, Beardsley and Goya.

1903 Founding of the Salon d'Automne in Paris.
Kandinsky makes a trip to Tunis and Kairouan.
Marc visits Paris for the first time.
Works by Cézanne, Gauguin, Van Gogh, Bonnard and Munch exhibited at the Berlin Secession.
Cassirer publishes the magazine "Kunst und Künstler" in Berlin.
First performance of Schönberg's "Verklärte Nacht" in Vienna.

1904 Neo-Impressionist exhibition organized by the Phalanx in Munich.
August Macke studies art at the Düsseldorf Academy.
Cézanne exhibits at the Salon d'Automne and in Berlin at Cassirer's.
Hodler Exhibition at the Vienna Secession.
Anton von Webern meets Schönberg and becomes his pupil.

1905 Takes to painting on glass. Short visit to Paris.

1905 Matisse begins "Luxe, calme et volupté."
The Fauves create a sensation at the Salon d'Automne in Paris.
Founding of the "Die Brücke" group in Dresden (Heckel, Kirchner, Schmidt-Rottluff, Bleyl).
Building of the Palais Stoclet in Brussels, designed by Hoffmann.

1906 Marries the pianist Lily Stumpf and settles in Munich. First etchings exhibited at the Munich Secession.

1906 Kandinsky works at Sèvres, near Paris.
Munch paints the third "Frieze of Life" for the foyer of the Berlin Schauspielhaus.
Death of Cézanne.

1907 Picasso finishes "Les Demoiselles d'Avignon" in Paris.
Brücke Exhibition at the Richter Gallery, Dresden.

1908 Influenced by Cézanne, Van Gogh and Ensor. Participates in the exhibitions of the Berlin and Munich Secession.

1908 Van Gogh exhibitions in Munich.
Wilhelm Worringer publishes "Abstraktion und Einfühlung."
Anton von Webern composes his "Passacaglia."

1909 Much impressed by the Hans von Marées exhibition at the Munich Secession.

> 1909 Works by Cézanne and Matisse exhibited at the Thannhauser Gallery, Munich.
> Founding of the Neue Münchener Künstlervereinigung, with Kandinsky as chairman.
> Marinetti publishes the Futurist Manifesto in "Le Figaro," Paris.

1910 The designer and illustrator Alfred Kubin visits Klee's studio and gives him encouragement. In October he exhibits 55 drawings, watercolors and etchings at the Kunsthaus, Zurich, and later at Bern and Basel.

> 1910 Balla, Boccioni, Carrà, Russolo and Severini sign the Manifesto of Futurist Painting in Milan.
> Macke and Marc become acquainted in Munich; the latter exhibits at the Brakl Gallery.
> Kandinsky's first abstract drawings and watercolors.
> The magazine "Der Sturm" launched in Berlin.
> Delaunay exhibits his "Eiffel Tower" at the Salon des Indépendants, Paris.

1911 First one-man show at the Thannhauser Gallery, Munich. Meets Macke, Marc, Jawlensky, Gabriele Münter, Marianne von Werefkin, Kandinsky. Sees pictures by Delaunay at the first Blaue Reiter Exhibition. Illustrates Voltaire's "Candide" with 25 drawings (published in 1920).

> 1911 Founding of "Der Blaue Reiter" in Munich.
> Kandinsky publishes "Über das Geistige in der Kunst," written the previous year.

1912 Takes part in the second Blaue Reiter Exhibition, devoted to graphic work, at the Goltz Gallery, Munich; other participants include Braque, Picasso, Derain, Vlaminck, Larionov, Malevitch and Gontcharova.
During a visit to Paris Klee meets Picasso, Wilhelm Uhde, Delaunay, Le Fauconnier and Apollinaire.

> 1912 Kandinsky and Marc publish the album entitled "Der Blaue Reiter."
> Delaunay exhibits "Simultaneous Windows" at the Salon des Indépendants, Paris.
> Arnold Schönberg composes "Pierrot Lunaire."

1913 Klee translates Delaunay's article "Sur la lumière" (Über das Licht), published in "Der Sturm," January 1913.
Spends part of the winter in Bern.

> 1913 Delaunay paints "Simultaneous Disks."
> The Armory Show takes place in New York.

1914 Founding member of the New Munich Secession. Trip to Tunis and Kairouan in April with August Macke and Louis Moilliet. Influenced by Cubism.

> 1914 The Munich art world broken up and scattered by the outbreak of war. Kandinsky returns to Russia. Macke killed in action. At the front Franz Marc fills a notebook with abstract sketches (Feldskizzenbuch).

> 1915 In Holland Mondrian paints his first pictures entirely in horizontals and verticals.

1916-1918 Serves in the German army behind the lines.

> 1916 Franz Marc killed in action at Verdun.

1917 Klee exhibits at the Dada Gallery in Zurich.

> 1917 Theo van Doesburg founds the review "De Stijl" at Leyden. Alban Berg begins work on "Wozzeck," an opera in three acts and fifteen scenes, finished in 1921.

1918 First illustrated monograph on Klee published by "Der Sturm," Berlin.

> 1919 Mondrian settles in Paris.
> At Weimar the architect Walter Gropius founds the Bauhaus; Feininger and Marcks join the teaching staff.
> Kandinsky appointed Professor of Fine Arts at the University of Moscow.

1920 May-June: retrospective exhibition at the Goltz Gallery, Munich (356 works).
Contributes his own "creative credo" to the anthology "Schöpferische Konfession."
Executes 10 lithographs for Curt Corrinth's book, "Potsdamer Platz, oder die Nächte des neuen Messias."
Walter Gropius offers him a professorship at the Weimar Bauhaus; Klee accepts and settles at Weimar in January 1921.

> 1920 In Paris Léonce Rosenberg publishes Mondrian's book "Le Néo-Plasticisme."

1921-1924 Klee teaches at the Weimar Bauhaus.

> 1921 Van Doesburg founds a "De Stijl" group at Weimar in close collaboration with the Bauhaus.
> In Moscow Kandinsky founds the Academy of the Arts and Sciences.
> Viking Eggeling and Hans Richter turn their first abstract film.

> 1922 Kandinsky and Moholy-Nagy join the teaching staff of the Bauhaus.
> Willi Baumeister decorates the Exhibition Hall in Stuttgart with mural paintings in relief.
> Schönberg publishes his "Harmonielehre."

1923 One-man show at the Kronprinzen-Palais, Berlin. Publishes an essay: "Wege des Naturstudiums" (Ways of Studying Nature).

> 1923 Le Corbusier publishes "Vers une architecture."
> In Germany Hans Richter, Mies van der Rohe and Werner Graeffe publish the magazine "G".

1924 First Klee Exhibition in New York at the Société Anonyme. In January, delivers a lecture at Jena. Founding of the group known as "Die Blaue Vier" (Kandinsky, Feininger, Jawlensky, Klee). In December Klee leaves the Bauhaus.

> 1924 André Breton publishes the Surrealist Manifesto in Paris.

1925 Klee publishes his "Pädagogisches Skizzenbuch" (Pedagogical Sketchbook). Second large-scale exhibition of his work at the Goltz Gallery, Munich. Takes part in the first general Surrealist Exhibition at the Galerie Pierre, Paris.

> 1925 The Bauhaus moves from Weimar to Dessau.
> Mondrian publishes "Die Neue Gestaltung."

1926 First one-man show in Paris. Becomes professor at the new Bauhaus in Dessau. Trip to Italy.

1928 Publishes "Exakte Versuche im Bereiche der Kunst" (Exact Experiments in the Field of Art).

> 1928 André Breton publishes "Le Surréalisme et la peinture."

1928 Visits Egypt for study purposes during the winter.
Summer stay in the South of France.

1929 International Exhibition of Abstract Art in Zurich.
Breton publishes the Second Surrealist Manifesto.
Bunuel and Dali produce the film "Un chien andalou."

1930 Klee Exhibition at the Museum of Modern Art, New York.

1930 Van Doesburg launches the review "Art Concret."
July: first number of the magazine "Le Surréalisme au service
de la révolution."

1931 Leaves the Dessau Bauhaus and accepts a professorship at the
Academy of Fine Arts, Düsseldorf.
Pictures inspired by Divisionism.
Trip to Sicily.

1932 The Bauhaus moves from Dessau to Berlin.
"Abstraction-Création" group founded in Paris (Mondrian,
Gabo, Pevsner, etc.).

1933 Leaves Germany at the end of the year and returns to Bern.

1933 The Nazis close down the Bauhaus. Schmidt-Rottluff and
Schlemmer are forced to give up their teaching posts in Berlin.
Schwitters leaves Germany for Oslo; Kandinsky settles in
Paris, Schönberg goes to the United States.

1935 Retrospective exhibition in Bern, Basel and Lucerne. First
symptoms of his illness.

1935 Death of Malevitch.

1937 In Germany 102 of Klee's works are confiscated by the Nazis,
and 17 of them figure in the exhibition of "degenerate art,"
Munich.
Braque and Picasso pay a visit to Klee in Switzerland.

1937 Feininger leaves Germany and returns to New York. Beck-
mann takes refuge in Amsterdam. Moholy-Nagy opens the
New Bauhaus in Chicago.
Picasso paints "Guernica."

1938 Klee Exhibitions in New York and Paris.

1940 Dies at Muralto-Locarno, Switzerland, June 29th.

PAUL KLEE

INTRODUCTION

IN June 1902 Paul Klee made the following entry in his diary: "Imagine quite a small formal motif and attempt a concise rendering of it; naturally not by easy stages but straightaway, in other words, armed with a pencil. That anyhow is a real action, and small reiterated acts will yield more in the end than poetic frenzy without form or arrangement... I'm learning from scratch, I'm beginning to build form as if I knew nothing at all about painting. For I have discovered a tiny undisputed property: a particular kind of three-dimensional representation on a flat surface." [1]

Klee was twenty-three at the time; his poetics were vague but already he was laying the foundations on which, in pursuance of his goal, he gradually raised the constructions of his imagination. And yet, so specific a statement of his aims, at a time when contemporary art had scarcely begun to achieve a vision of its own, takes on an extraordinary importance in retrospect, in so far as it seems to anticipate, by so many years, certain ideas which lie at the origin of some of the most recent trends of art. His words, in fact, lay stress on the importance of the act, and therefore on the human reality of the artist, who is enabled to exteriorize himself, to realize himself ("realize" precisely in the sense of making real), in the empirical experience of action. We need not be led astray by Klee's express desire "to know nothing at all about painting." His emotion sprang from a direct approach to objects, to nature, an approach bordering at times on a happy abandonment, indeed on a boyish vein of satire, but always this close contact with things had its origin in a deep plenitude made up of mature human passions and expressed with an absolute mastery of the painter's medium, a medium which always formed an integral part of his artistic experience. Klee himself in later years was very

CHILDHOOD DRAWING: SCENE WITH HARE, 1884. COLOR CRAYON.
KLEE FOUNDATION, BERN.

explicit on this point: "The legend of the childishness of my drawing must have its origin in those linear pictures in which I tried to combine the objective representation of, let us say, a man with a pure presentation of the linear element... Besides, I don't want to render man as he is, but as he might be." [2]

From the outset, the problem was that of interpreting, freely and naturalistically, the reality and essence of man. Without evading the issue, of course, but on the other hand without limiting his own poetic world to such an interpretation. And his contacts with contemporary experiments in painting proved to be fruitful for Klee inasmuch as they helped him to achieve independence with respect to the purely contingent vision of reality; in this he stood in full agreement with the main trend of art in the Europe of his time. "Not unlike James Joyce," writes Carola Giedion-Welcker, [3] "he was an individualist, remaining aloof from all artistic alliances." The comparison is apt and telling. Like Joyce, Klee seems to create his language independently of any tradition and, above all, outside of any known modality. Syntactically and lexically, his language has an original modulation of its own, which takes account of no pre-existing rule but only of its own immediate necessities of expression. It must not be forgotten, however, that the formulation of this language was rendered possible by a European climate of inquiry and investigation, which inevitably affected the collateral experiments undertaken by Klee. Notwithstanding the desire expressed in 1902 to "build form as if I knew nothing at all about painting" —and obviously the painting he repudiated was that of a European tradition which had become burdensome and stultifying—the fact remains that Klee's training and development as an artist took place in the most European climate possible. Not even the war could succeed in destroying this community of ideas and research work, if not of achievement, and the Bauhaus for example, of which Klee became an active member, arose precisely as a united effort of fraternal collaboration in the European sense; it might even be said that it was the last attempt to save a Europe committed, unconsciously and irrationally, to its own destruction.

Spontaneously, out of an inner necessity, Klee moved in the direction leading to complete autonomy of pictorial language, free from any naturalistic reference of too urgent a nature, because the very objects he presents lose the value of naturalistic forms and assume rather a fantastic quality. And driven by the same necessity to isolate and create forms, the artist at times achieved an absolutely geometrical formulation of his compositions.

It is certainly true that Klee's steady course of development from his early figurative work to his experiments in abstraction—and for him abstraction did not necessarily preclude a figurative image—was in many ways similar to Kandinsky's parallel course. Yet it must be borne in mind that between Klee and Kandinsky, even within the limits of similar taste, there were notable differences. Kandinsky is distinguished from Klee in this, that for him it was impossible to revert to a concurrence, even *a posteriori*, of the created form with its phenomenological aspect: the reaction to what he himself called materialism, and which at bottom he identified with the whole previous history of art, came as a deliberate rejection of apparent reality. The *Stimmung* of the moment, concord with a given psychic atmosphere, was enough, Kandinsky felt, to lift art and the artist above material contingencies into the *Geistige*, the spiritual. But this yearning for intensity and sublimation was still part and parcel of Romanticism; Kandinsky, that is to say, had reached the critical juncture of romantic idealism, but he showed no interest in going beyond that point. On this account his lesson was learned more easily than that of Klee, who, having gone beyond, has an importance whose full scope has yet to be realized, and which has come to bear on the most recent trends of non-figurative painting. Indeed, in Klee the absolute freedom of the sign appears as a configuration of the world from which, however, the sense of human society is by no means excluded, and the will to create is at the same time a will to participate in the social life, indeed is a necessary contribution to the life of contemporary society.

For Klee, then, the problem of reality is more complex. For him there can be no question of a short and simple repudiation of it. Nor, moreover, can it be immobilized and suspended in space and time, cut off from sensations, as it is in the concept of *constant reality* expressed and realized by Mondrian in conjunction with the experiments of the De Stijl group. It may be said, on the contrary, that for Klee reality is never motionless and therefore never constant. It resides, first of all, in the work of art and not in the relationship of the pictorial image with the external image—this may be included but is not indispensable—but on the other hand it involves all the rational and irrational activity of the artist, his visual experience and his psychic experience, and is thus the exteriorization and plastic realization of the active complexity of the individual, without excluding any moment or any sensation; in a word, it is subject to a continuous variation which, though determined by experience —experience of acts, of feelings, of perceptions—cannot be reduced to a two-dimensional neo-plasticism (Mondrian), even less to the rejection and negation of materiality (Kandinsky).

In the handling of pure graphic and pictorial means Klee found the fully coherent expression that most closely approximated to the modalities of his world, and to his capacity for living and feeling in that world. Some have spoken of "fables" in connection with his painting, but the word fails to apply when taken to mean merely an avenue of escape, a dream of life that does not exist, a means of evading the reality of one's own condition. This can have no bearing on an experience so wholeheartedly entered into, and so closely bound up, historically and dramatically, with the crisis of a whole civilization. The very cultural tendencies with which Klee allied himself, first a certain type of Jugendstil, then Expressionism, later his private form of Surrealism, and even the assimilation of as much of Cubism and Neo-Plasticism as could serve his purpose, go to show how deeply rooted the artist was in his own time, and how exact a correspondence there was between his means of expression and his human situation. Yet no sign is arbitrary, no color is applied by chance, no image is fanciful; all are real forms, of a reality which undergoes no imposition from without, which may or may not have a connection with naturalistic reality, but which is always autonomous.

German Expressionism, above all that of the Brücke group, was the last filiation with Romanticism. The Expressionism of the Blaue Reiter was the focal point of the crisis of Romanticism, its final consequence and the initial reaction against it. Klee, in all his experience, maintained this reaction, steadily and consistently carrying it toward a repudiation of romantic and late romantic canons. Above all, after the tragedy of the First World War, it was no longer possible for an artist conscious of his historical position to temporize with what had gone before or to resume the thread of his discourse where it had been broken off. Society was recovering from a crisis which it had proved quite incapable of resolving, and was moving toward an even more terrible crisis, which burst out in 1939, but which had already been acute throughout the thirties. Klee lived through all these years of anguish: the language he worked out for himself, a language of signs, lines and colors, answered not only to the necessities of his imagination, but to the anguish of his conscience. It was a language worked out within the framework of a precise and conscious human condition, that of the dialectical relationship between the artist and society, between man and his history. To give form to all this meant creating one of the most genuine, most representative expressions of art of our civilization.

FROM BERN TO MUNICH

PAUL KLEE was born at Münchenbuchsee, near Bern, on December 18, 1879. In a *curriculum vitae* written in 1940 [4] the artist himself tells us about his childhood and schooling. "My father was a music master at the Cantonal Teachers' College of Hofwyl; my mother was Swiss. When I started school in the spring of 1886, we lived in the Länggasse, Bern. I attended the first four classes of the local primary school. Then my parents sent me to the municipal grammar school, where I completed the four classes and then went on to study the humanities in the same institution. Passing the Cantonal examinations, I graduated in the autumn of 1898. This concluded my general education. Choosing my profession proved easy enough, outwardly at least. While every career was open to me thanks to my graduation certificate, I decided to try my luck at studying art and, if I succeeded, to make painting my life's work. To carry out such a plan at that time—and the same is largely true today—meant going abroad. The choice lay between Paris and Germany. Temperamentally I was more attracted by Germany. So I set out for the Bavarian capital, where the Art Academy referred me to the private preparatory school run by Knirr. There I studied drawing and painting, and before long entered the class of Franz Stuck at the Academy."

This biographical sketch, mere sketch though it is, is enough for us to trace the early path followed by the artist. But apart from his actual training as a painter, it must not be forgotten that Paul Klee also received a musical education of great importance in the development of his artistic taste. His father, a German, was a singing master. His Swiss mother had studied music at the Stuttgart Conservatory. Will Grohmann, in his fundamental study of Klee, writes: "Still more significant than this interaction of painting and poetry is the way Klee mingled

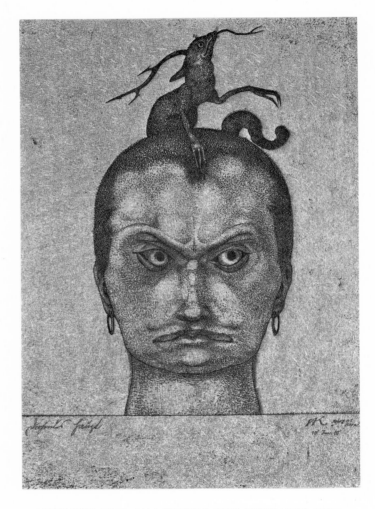

MENACING HEAD, 1905. ETCHING. KLEE FOUNDATION, BERN.

painting and music. He was an excellent musician himself, often playing for his own enjoyment, and never at a loss to read and interpret a score. Though he did not compose, he thoroughly understood the process of musical composition and was as much at home with Igor Stravinsky's musical system as with Arnold Schönberg's twelve-tone scale. Bach, Mozart, and Haydn were as familiar to him as the poems of Goethe to poetry lovers, and he knew practically every one of their works..." [5]

One might go even further: Klee's painting becomes at times the graphic transcription of a musical rhythm, not only in the abstract sense of rhythmic caesuras, of musicality infused in the pictorical image, but in the more concrete sense of transposing a musical ideogram into a pictorial dimension. In other words, Klee not only readily grasped the meaning of sound, but was able to individualize its structure. That music for him could have a graphic equivalent is shown, in one instance among others, by a transposition which he carried out on the basis of a score by Johann Sebastian Bach: the pitch of the sounds, the pauses, the chromatic texture of the score are transformed into a script which tends to have not only the same meaning, but even to achieve the same rhythm and tempo, the same dimension which now is no longer physical. His paintings, however, even when their titles are couched in musical terms, were never inspired by the musical sentiment of others; the sensation underlying them was always autonomous, and always expressed with purely graphic and pictorial means in a dimension above and beyond the three traditional ones, a dimension in which it could also exist as purity of sound. And—to pursue a simile which, moreover, has its historical justification—it is precisely on this account that Klee's artistic culture goes beyond an experience such as that of Stravinsky, or even of Schönberg, to establish and define a new, distinct, but actively present dimension, more akin to the music of Anton von Webern.

It was in his maturity of course that Klee achieved all this, in the years in which he lived through, and contributed to bring about, a renewal of European culture. But his early years, as he buckled down to his early pictorial experiments, almost exclusively graphic, were a time of apprenticeship, without any revolt as yet against the codified tradition of Central Europe. The trajectory of these early experiments runs essentially from Central European realism to Jugendstil. The spontaneity and ingenuous fancy of the early drawings of his childhood lie, logically enough, outside the bounds of tradition; but the realism of his subsequent drawings, more accomplished, more deliberately committed in a given direction, definitely falls in line with tradition. Until he went to Munich in 1898, Klee had no very decided preferences, and the tradition to which he stood nearest may have been that of Swiss painting. Of Hodler for example, but certainly not so much the Hodler of the large mural compositions as the one we find in some of the small landscapes. Or again, to go back further into the 19th century, he may have been acquainted with the drawings of artists like Freudenberger, a Bernese painter, drawings and engravings of a sentimental, minutely detailed realism, but technically skillful and rapid, suggestively shrouded in a certain vague atmosphere. The realism of Klee's early drawings, however, is less sentimental. He sought to capture the appearance of the visual world, to record it, and through that record to attain a more lasting sensation. Hence the preoccupations that show him overcoming the realistic rendering of landscape and figures in the drawings of 1895-1897. Even when the drawing is a genre scene, a vein of caricatural, satirical notation always enters into it which at times amounts to a pre-expressionist distortion.

The character of this distortion, and the almost implacable spirit behind it, must be borne in mind when considering Klee's subsequent activity in the Munich art world at the end of the 19th century. It was a milieu that had been strongly affected by the innovations of Art Nouveau, which took its rise in Belgium and turned into Jugendstil in Germany, after a transition which had already lessened its quality. Yet the originality of Klee's intentions is clear even in such a milieu. The studies he made at Knirr's preparatory school cannot really be called academic studies. Obviously the course of instruction followed traditional lines, the nude, the elements of the human body, studies of heads and arms; but all this, in Klee's drawings, lies outside the classical canons. Even though the modeling is static, forms gain animation from a line that glides swiftly and surely. In the few paintings made at that time, the composition, being intended to bring out the forms and features of objects, is accordingly more realistic; but it is a realism that breaks off in particular details and little by little acquires a stylistic significance of its own, which is no longer limited merely to the direct observation of things and to the transcription of them. However, Klee did not achieve this originality in the significant use of the sign and compositional line until such time as he had assimilated not only the linearism of Jugendstil, but also that of collateral experiments.

The trip to Italy he made in 1901 with the Swiss sculptor Hermann Haller came as the revelation of a new world, indeed of a new light experienced among the monuments of every age, from mosaics to frescos and architecture. Artistically Klee seemed to derive no immediate benefit from it all. Actually, however, it was precisely this sense of the solar qualities, the sunniness of images and colors, that he was to seek for and retrieve thirteen years later, during his trip to North Africa. But in the meantime his painting remained rooted in the realism of Central Europe, in the Secessionist elements which appear more clearly than ever before in the *Portrait of the Artist's Sister* of 1903 (Klee Foundation, Bern). For one like Klee, who had lived outside the currents of French art, it was logical to hark back to Secessionist linearism, even making no allowance for the instruction he received from Franz Stuck. As with Gustav Klimt about the same time, line with Klee served to build up an image meant to be, in so far as possible, autonomous. Up to this time Klee had worked without any knowledge of the conquests of light and space made by French Impressionism and Post-Impressionism. His evasion of visual reality, whenever he did evade it, thus retained a wholly literary savor. And this trend persisted in the engravings which Klee carried out in these years and which culminated in several famous works, regarded by some as the key to his painting of later years. These engravings were executed between 1902 and his first trip to Paris in 1905. The emphatic symbolism of images like the *Virgin in a Tree*, the *Comedian*, the *Hero with a Wing*, is expressed in terms of the traditional graphic means, with elementary contrasts of light and shade, which nevertheless succeed in lifting the symbolism, still all too literary, to a super-real plane, which is not that of a *divertissement* or a fable, however, but often amounts to social satire or a parody of manners.

Klee by this time had discovered the masters of the satirical and fantastic, and on them he fixed his choice and his attention in the years between 1903 and 1905: William Blake, Aubrey Beardsley and, greatest of them all, Goya. If Klee had had behind him the French tradition of Impressionism and Post-Impressionism, he might have made his way back to the painting of Goya much sooner. Now, as it so happened, it was Goya's powerful vein of satire and caricature—always, however, committed to the service of a cause—which led him to study the Spanish master in the etchings of the *Caprichos* and in the distortions of the *Disasters of War*. But when we allow for the all too often literary quality of Central European realism, we realize too the importance Blake's fantastic constructions and

GROUP OF TREES, 1899. OIL. KLEE FOUNDATION, BERN.

Beardsley's decorative fantasies must have had for the young Swiss artist. His attachment to them was not the result of an accidental encounter: what Klee was looking for—and this is borne out by the entry in his diary quoted above—was an autonomy of painting, an autonomy of the pictorial image, to put it more precisely, such as did not rule out a constant relationship with society. This relationship, in the early engravings, is still too patently literary, but it is obvious that the lesson

PORTRAIT OF THE ARTIST'S SISTER, 1903. OIL.
KLEE FOUNDATION, BERN.

they embody is derived from a tradition, like that of the English artists, which, though it concedes a good deal to literary inspiration, nevertheless retains an autonomy of image, above all an autonomy of concept, which is not to be met with elsewhere in European art, anyhow not before Impressionism. *Menacing Head*, etched by Klee in 1905, has a direct connection with *The Cat*, executed by Beardsley in 1895, a connection almost iconographical. Yet there are notable differences between the two works, because inspired at different times and, above all, based on different compositional schemes. Beardsley seems to make play with the white of the woman's head below, out of which the black cat rises like a fantastic apparition, defined by a thin white outline against an equally black background. Already Klee shows a desire for a new compositional order, more rational than hitherto, in the clean break of the compositional plane by means of a horizontal line, in an expressive accentuation obtained by the convergence of the eyes, in the disproportionate elongation of the mouth. Klee's composition is a fanciful one no doubt, but it is justified by a pictorial reality and thus loses that decorative character which persists in Beardsley's work. Klee, indeed, might be said to stress the emotive content of the image, an emotivity still too subjective and undetached to be universal, but obviously it was just such a composition as this that enabled Klee to overcome the linearism of Jugendstil and to charge form with a significance frankly verging now on Expressionism.

It is true that the linearism of Jugendstil, its concern with harmonic curves rather than with a resolute grouping of constructive masses, has its parallel not only in Beardsley but in certain paintings of Toorop and Khnopff, in the grotesque masquerades of the early Ensor. But it is also true that, in painting and above all in graphic work, Jugendstil stands close to the work of one of the precursors of expressionist painting: Edvard Munch. But his was an art, it has been rightly pointed out, that seems rather to mark an end than to initiate a new order or awaken a new sensibility. Klee's case of course is quite different: he was really in search of a new order and a new sensibility. Just about the time Klee arrived in Munich, in 1897-1898, August Endell was building his Elvira Studio, one of the major achievements of Jugendstil and undoubtedly Endell's most famous work. As we look at it, we realize how allusively symbolic its decoration is, inspired by naturalistic elements but transfigured by the necessity of adapting everything to a fanciful, abstract rhythm. The main stylistic lines of the work were stressed by Endell in the treatise he published in 1898. Klee chose to go another way, even though, naturally enough, he was to remain strongly impressed by the achievements of Jugendstil, above all by the cultural climate created at Munich by such personalities as Endell, Hermann Obrist and Otto Eckmann. Klee's line never lost its function of expressive accentuation, and thus avoided the dreamy, decorative languors of so much of the art of the period.

Certainly in these early experiments in the grotesque, on which Ensor too probably had some influence, we are still within the bounds of a romantic sensibility; even more than a sensation, Klee sought to express an ideal that had taken shape in his mind, like a superstructure, as it were. It is not at all a literary ideal, but a coherent and continuous search for the means of expression that were to be peculiarly his own, for they had to have a complexity capable of expressing the totality of his ideas, if not yet of his sensations.

In his diary, in 1902, Klee specified his aims as follows: "I can hardly bear the thought of having to live in a period of mere imitation in the arts. In Italy I was almost hopelessly resigned to the thought. Now, in actual practice, I am trying to disregard all this and to build modestly on my own, without looking either right or left.

"There are three things at the present time: Greco-Roman antiquity *(physis)* with an objective outlook, worldly aims and architectonic emphasis, and Christianity *(psyche)* with a subjective outlook, otherworldly aims and musical emphasis. The third consists in being modest, ignorant and self-taught, a tiny Ego." [6]

This lucidity of mind, this consciousness of his own limits, is amazing in so young an artist. But it was just this lucidity that never deserted him throughout the experience of a lifetime, and enabled him to stand firm through a major crisis of society and social institutions, while reacting to it with the creation of a body of work unimpaired by any crisis, because it came as the fruit of a continuous search for harmony between his own sensibility, his own imagination, and his own way of life in the world. Thus it was even possible for him to carry over the boldest soundings of the subconscious into a rational sphere of expression in which he sought to mend the break that had developed with society. By this time, in the early years of the 20th century, the conviction of an inner compulsion guiding his work had taken hold of the artist, with the result that he had resolved to create a style of his own, not abstracted from the sensibility of his own condition, hence not decorative; a style far removed from Jugendstil, bound up with the world and society, suited to expressing his sensibility and his sense of contemporary history. The artist was now ready to take his place in the vanguard of European painting, to assimilate its conquests and contribute to its expansion, helping to broaden its confines and open up unsuspected horizons.

STREET WITH CARRIAGE, 1907. GLASS PAINTING.
FRANK LAURENS COLLECTION, CINCINNATI, OHIO.

THE EUROPEAN VANGUARD

IN 1905 Klee began experimenting with a new technique, that of painting on glass, and in the same year produced his *Garden Scene with a Watering Can* (Felix Klee Collection, Bern) in this medium. He made a trip to Paris, but without any immediate effect on his work; it was only later that he discovered and investigated the significance of the adventurous achievements of French painting in these years. His *Garden Scene* is wholly subordinated to the realistic interpretation of the motif, with rapid jottings whose movement is accentuated by color. There is, however, a rigorous attempt at spatial organization, virtually a subdivision of the picture into zones and an abrupt cutting off of the composition which serves to increase the effectiveness of the representation. There is still an almost hedonistic contemplation of the image, of objects and things, and a feeling of uncertainty as to the pictorial suitability of these images. His other glass pictures show a tendency toward the grotesque.

In 1906 he married the pianist Lily Stumpf and settled down for good in Munich. These were the years in which Expressionism was undergoing a transformation, moving away from the literary toward the abstract, not only as regards the figurative arts; the composition of Arnold Schönberg's *Pierrot Lunaire*, remember, dates from 1912. Klee, an eager observer of the evolution of all the arts, keenly interested, needless to say, in that of music, felt the need to attain to an immediacy of language, to what in music was called the *Urlaut*, and which had to be expressed in the sonorous outcry of color, in order to achieve a *sense of form*. In 1909 Schönberg wrote in his *Harmonielehre*: "When I compose, I decide only through feeling, through a sense of form. This tells me what I should write, everything else is ruled out. Every chord I write corresponds to an inner compulsion: to a compulsion exerted by my need for expression, but also perhaps to an inexorable but unconscious logic of harmonic construction." [7]

Street with Carriage (Frank Laurens Collection, Cincinnati) is a glass picture painted in 1907. The realistic notation loses its descriptive significance; the emotion remains linked with form and not with the genre scene; the carriage, the shadows, the fence, all assume the value of a peculiar chromatic pitch in accordance with "an inexorable but unconscious logic of harmonic construction." *Street with Carriage* probably contains an echo of the formal violence of certain compositions of Munch, but from now on Klee was seeking his preferences elsewhere. The influences discernible in the works he showed at the 1908 Secession exhibition in Munich and Berlin are still disparate, but his discovery of Van Gogh was beginning to bear fruit. If there was something to be gained from Expressionism, Klee preferred to go back to the fountainhead for it. Through Van Gogh he succeeded in overcoming every other pictorial influence, that of Hans von Marées for example, whose frescos in the Aquarium at Naples had been admired by Klee during his trip to Italy in 1901. Two Van Gogh exhibitions were held at Munich in 1908; at the same time Klee became acquainted with the Impressionists thanks to the works that Hugo von Tschudi was collecting for the German museums. The following year he was able to study works by Cézanne and Matisse in exhibitions held at the Thannhauser Gallery.

Van Gogh opened Klee's eyes to the power of non-decorative line to build, to do violence to form, to define it in a dimension that was no longer naturalistic. The goal pursued, but with much greater effectiveness of presentation and much more emotional power, was still that of achieving a *sense of form*. From Cézanne he learned how to give order to sensations, how to make them universal and enduring, eluding traditionally

GARDEN SCENE WITH A WATERING CAN, 1905. WATERCOLOR ON GLASS.
FELIX KLEE COLLECTION, BERN.

accepted laws of time, to express them in terms of an emotional
constant, beyond the limits of three-dimensional space, in a new
constructive order. From Matisse—even before he became
acquainted with Delaunay's work—Klee learned the free
handling of color, the juxtaposition of primary tones, with a
view to greater pictorial effectiveness in presenting images
through the "shock on our senses," as Matisse himself put it.

THE ARTIST AT THE WINDOW (SELF-PORTRAIT), 1909.
INK WASH AND COLORED CHALK. FELIX KLEE COLLECTION, BERN.

Girl with Jugs (1910, Felix Klee Collection, Bern), not a glass picture but an oil painting, still harbors a certain expressionism in the violence with which the image is presented, but form unfolds more calmly. Klee liberates his sign and organizes it in terms of a volumetric definition of forms, tilted upward toward the picture surface: a bold compositional device not to be found in his earlier work. Equally bold is his handling of color. Indeed, it is color above all else which has gone beyond mere naturalism and achieved autonomy here; and though not yet capable of attaining to an organic construction, it is certainly better organized than it was in the self-portrait of the previous year, known as *The Artist at the Window* (Felix Klee Collection, Bern), still charged to the full with expressionist violence.

The year 1911 was an important one in Klee's life: it was the year in which the Blue Rider (Der Blaue Reiter) was founded. In 1909 a group of artists, among them Kandinsky, Kubin, Jawlensky and Gabriele Münter, had formed the New Association of Munich Artists (Neue Münchener Künstlervereinigung) with a view to bringing together the youthful energies of the Munich art world at that time. But the Association had no well-defined program, no unifying aims, and very soon fell apart, as the divergencies existing between its members led each artist to go his own way. In 1911 Franz Marc (who had just joined the Association) and Kandinsky prepared a volume entitled *Der Blaue Reiter* in which the new esthetic theories were set forth and illustrated. On December 18, 1911, at the Thannhauser Gallery, Kandinsky, Kubin, Marc and Gabriele Münter, who had now all withdrawn from the New Association of Munich Artists, opened the first Blaue Reiter exhibition, alongside artists of other countries, like the Douanier Rousseau, Robert Delaunay and others; the German painter Macke and the composer Schönberg also took part. Three months later the Blaue Reiter group organized a second exhibition, of graphic art, at the Goltz Gallery, which this time included works by Braque, Picasso, Derain and Vlaminck, and the Russians Larionov, Malevitch and Natalie Gontcharova. Klee was represented at this exhibition, which brought together some of the most advanced painters in Europe.

In 1911 Klee had made the acquaintance of Kandinsky and the other painters of his circle, and the friendship that sprang up between them undoubtedly contributed to clarify Klee's own ideas. In December of the same year Kandinsky had published his essay, *Über das Geistige in der Kunst (On the Spiritual in Art)*, written in 1910. The Blaue Reiter grew out of the rising trend toward Expressionism, but it was a way of seeing which neither overlooked nor belittled the recent conquests of contemporary figurative experiments. By means of a dynamic accentuation of forms, carried in the direction of abstraction and obtained through a direct knowledge of the work of the Fauves and Cubists, the artists of the Blaue Reiter group were able to achieve what they set out to do: to transcend form itself and to simplify it with a view to magnifying its emotive content. The resulting pictorial style constituted a definitive advance on the expressionism that lay at the origin of it. The expressionism in question had in fact been that of the Brücke, whose motifs Kandinsky had been trying to take over at the time the New Association of Munich Artists was founded, and which evolved toward abstraction in the hands of the Blaue Reiter group. Marc, Macke and Kandinsky himself were all moving on to the plane of non-figurative abstraction, beyond the range of Cubism itself. "We have no intention of advocating any precise or particular form," they wrote in the catalogue of the first Blaue Reiter exhibition. "Our aim is to show, in the variety of forms represented, how the artist's innermost desire takes shape in many different ways." [8] And in his essay *On the Spiritual in Art* Kandinsky dwelt on the sense of inner necessity which

GIRL WITH JUGS, 1910. OIL.
FELIX KLEE COLLECTION, BERN.

drives the artist on, the same emotional compulsion Schönberg had spoken of in connection with music: "Color is the keyboard. The eye is the hammer, while the soul is a piano of many strings. The artist is the hand which, through the medium of different keys, causes the human soul to vibrate. Thus it is evident that color harmony can rest only on the principle of the corresponding vibration of the human soul. This basis can be considered as *the principle of innermost necessity.*" [9]

Something has already been said of the extent to which Klee and Kandinsky differed, both in temperament and in their outlook on the world. For Klee the problem of reality was not to be solved by a simple rejection of the tangible world, with the resultant search for a spirituality of form above and beyond the materialism of phenomenological appearances. The solution, he felt, lay in working out the relationship between the complexity of the artist, of his visual and psychological reactions to the tangible world, and the consciousness of his own activity in a stylistic dimension which has its connections with the reality of external phenomena, but which may also transcend it in the structuralization of the composition, of the sign, of color and light. Accordingly, the drawings Klee made in these years betray none of the careful inquiry into the natural significance of things that marked the earlier ones, but increasingly break away from determinism, from the contingent, and take shape as autonomous images. From his illustrations for Voltaire's *Candide*, he moved on to the absolute freedom of such a drawing as *The Fleeing Policemen* (1913, Klee Foundation, Bern).

Some of the ideas expressed by Kandinsky had a fundamental importance for Klee because they coincided, anyhow up to a point, with the drift of his own researches. "Form alone can exist in its own right as the representation of an object (real or unreal) or as the purely abstract delimitation of space or surface," wrote Kandinsky. [10] Such an idea as this, with a few slight adjustments, Klee might have made his own. It is true, on the other hand, that Kandinsky's fund of experience in 1911 was much richer than Klee's, though the trend of the latter's work was no less clearly defined. And yet Klee was not satisfied. His trip to Paris in 1912, where he met Delaunay and saw works by Braque and Picasso, made him more keenly alive to the significance inherent in the compositional organization of the sign and of light. The chromatic vivacity of Delaunay's work had undoubtedly exercised a strong attraction on the artists of the Blaue Reiter group, but now, in the sixteen days he spent in Paris, in the many discussions he had with Delaunay, Klee realized the extent to which the necessity of organizing and energizing color had governed the experiments of the French artist. These, moreover, were the years when Cubism itself was moving toward that chromatic enrichment of surfaces which led up to the outbursts of Synthetic Cubism.

Klee took a keen interest in Delaunay's theories. For the review *Der Sturm*, which published it in January 1913, he made a German translation of Delaunay's essay *Sur la lumière*, written in the summer of 1912. Klee's eyes were to be fully opened to the emotive and imaginative power of color, in the sense of illumination, during his trip to Tunis in 1914, but meanwhile Delaunay's analyses of light and color were absorbed in his cultural make-up and contributed to his visual education. Light and color, he realized, had to be detached from every descriptive frame of reference, had to be handled with the same autonomy accorded to form. "Color cannot be extended indefinitely," Kandinsky had written. [11] But as Klee saw it, the physical limits of color might be overcome or pushed back to a psychological limit, with a corresponding gain in breadth of application. "Light reaches us by way of the sensibility," wrote Delaunay, and concluded: "For art to attain to the limit of sublimity, it has to approximate to our harmonic vision:

1913 55 Die fliehenden Polizisten

THE FLEEING POLICEMEN, 1913. PEN DRAWING.
KLEE FOUNDATION, BERN.

to clarity. Clarity lies in color and proportion; these proportions are made up of different, simultaneous measurements in an action. This action must be the representative harmony, the synchromatic movement (simultaneity) of light, which is the only reality." [12] And Klee also investigated the meaning of movement, of the simultaneous projection of sensations. He was familiar with the work of the Italian Futurists, which admittedly failed to influence him to the extent it influenced other German artists, but which nevertheless impressed him as one of the conquests of the new pictorial language.

It is significant that in 1908 there appeared in Germany the work of a philosopher who expounded a new theory of esthetics: *Abstraktion und Einfühlung (Abstraction and Empathy)*, by Wilhelm Worringer. His view of esthetics went far to justify the new trend toward non-figurative art which was gaining ground all over Europe. Worringer's book, which as a matter of fact was the thesis he submitted for his doctor's degree, was widely discussed in the Munich art world and unquestionably contributed in very large measure to diffuse the artistic culture represented by Klee and his friends, orienting it in precisely the direction they intended to pursue.

Worringer singled out a dual compulsion in man which art satisfies: empathy (*Einfühlung*, "feeling into") and abstraction. "The need of empathy can be regarded as underlying artistic expression only when the artist tends toward the organically life-like, that is, toward naturalism in the higher sense of the term... The recollection of the dead form of a pyramid, or of the repression of life, as manifested for example in Byzantine mosaics, tells us at once that here the need of empathy, which for obvious reasons always tends toward the organic, cannot possibly have determined the artist's intentions. The idea then forces itself upon us that here we have an impulse which is diametrically opposed to the impulse toward empathy, and which indeed seeks to repress everything that goes to satisfy the need of empathy. This opposite pole to the need of empathy appears to us to be the urge to abstraction." [13]

Later, in 1920, both in theory and practice, Klee personally experienced the urge to abstraction and found in it one of the necessities, one of the needs of his art. Meanwhile, in the years before 1914, his creative work shows him progressively breaking free of the strictly naturalistic approach—an approach too closely bound up with a form of determinism that amounted to a "repression of life" but not to a negation of it. At most it might be described as a check imposed on an over-exuberant vitality, that romantically surging vitality which underlies Expressionism, for example, and which accordingly culminated in an exuberant play of colors and forms and indeed in an intensification of the external dynamics of the composition. Klee felt that this exuberance had to be kept under control, and form and color made to fulfill a definite "function"; the link with visual reality subsisted, but rather in the nature of a dialectical exchange gradually leading up to an elaboration of the data of perception, very different from a tame acceptance of them. This, as we have seen, was the major concern of European art in these years, in all fields of expression, whether pictorial, literary or musical. The 20th century repudiated contemplation and put the accent on participation; artists were called upon to contribute to the making of a new culture, throwing themselves into it with a will, not merely allowing it to arise around them while they looked on passively. It was a sort of neo-humanism which, however, had lost faith in canons and conventions. It was an avant-garde movement which, appearances notwithstanding, inherited the thought of preceding centuries and enlisted it in the service of a permanent revolution which, again and again, as it gathers strength, issues a fresh challenge to complacency.

SPACE AND COLOR

"No more work for now. It's all pouring into me so deeply and gently, I can feel it and am gaining confidence, without any effort. Color has taken hold of me. I don't have to chase after it. It's got hold of me for good, I know. That is the meaning of this happy hour: color and I are one. I'm a painter." [14] Such was Klee's reaction to the light and color of North Africa at the time of his first trip to Tunis in 1914. His palette brightened up and came to life, and his colors, more mercurial and vibrant than ever before, played over forms with a new delicacy and refinement. The sunny, many-colored South, the vivid crowds at Tunis, the white buildings against the blue of sky and sea at Sidi-bou-Saïd, the virulence of the Mediterranean light in the port of Hammamet, the hill of Carthage from which the eye wanders out to the sea horizon—all this not only constituted a new visual experience, but came as the discovery of an altogether different way of life, of a new relationship between man and nature. Klee did not go to Africa in search of the romantically picturesque; a century after Delacroix this was hardly possible. But it was himself alone, his individuality, his painter's eye—"I'm a painter," he asserted with decision— that elicited the colored rhythms of the domes of the mosques at Kairouan and the color planes of the gardens near Tunis.

Klee landed in Tunis on April 7, 1914, accompanied by his friends Louis Moilliet and August Macke. He had fallen ill in Bern at the end of 1913, then had returned to Munich, where he helped to found the New Munich Secession, a rather shapeless concourse of artists which both Kandinsky and Franz Marc refused to join. The trip to Tunis afforded him an opportunity of testing out a new compositional structure and intensifying the autonomy of his pictorial language independently now of expressionist modulations.

BEFORE THE GATES OF KAIROUAN, 1914. WATERCOLOR.
KLEE FOUNDATION, BERN.

The watercolors in which Macke embodied his Tunisian impressions are very different from Klee's. Macke pursued the investigations of color which he had begun at the time the Blaue Reiter was founded; the new images he now created corresponded to a style that had already taken form; and even though his color was more brightly kindled now, it implemented a rhythm that had been consciously worked out well before. Klee, for his part, went south determined to embrace what he intuitively felt to be almost within his grasp, but had not yet succeeded in expressing fully. He knew what he had to do, but in order to achieve it he had to surrender to the "meaning of the hour." When he reached Tunis Klee already seemed to know what he had to look for and where to find it: not the external constructive features of the African coast, even less the picturesqueness of the landscape in its contrasts of white and blue; but the more impalpable and abstract element of that landscape. "Green, yellow, terracotta. The note strikes deep and will stay with me, even if I don't do any painting on the spot." [15] Color, construed as light and as a means of accentuating and strengthening the structure of the composition, was the conclusion Klee reached in the search he had begun from the very moment of his first contacts with the artists of the avant-garde; and it was the affirmation of his maturity as both an artist and a man, the definitive conquest of a pictorial language better suited, anyhow for Klee, to expressing the entire meaning of the human condition and the world as affecting him personally. And these were months of intense work, of increasingly subtle, increasingly exact approximations to his goal, until the war upset everything and scattered the ranks of the European vanguard, shattering the edifice of human reason and with it man's faith in man.

Before the Gates of Kairouan (1914, Klee Foundation, Bern) is a watercolor of disconcerting novelty as compared with the work of the previous year. Yet it too is the fruit of a maturing of the premises laid down at the time of his second trip to Paris, in 1912, seconded by the discovery of light as revealed by Delaunay and of space as revealed in Picasso's work. The color scheme of the composition is punctuated throughout by highly subtle tonal values, whose preciosity is emphasized by a technique of which Klee was now fully master, but at the same time the structural organization answers to a rhythm which

HOMAGE TO PICASSO, 1914. OIL.
PETER A. RÜBEL COLLECTION, COS COB, CONNECTICUT.

RED AND WHITE DOMES, 1914. WATERCOLOR. ▶
CLIFFORD ODETS COLLECTION, NEW YORK.

seems to be almost geometrical. Space, then, is organized in terms of surfaces, in a perspective that recedes along a single plane, even though the preciosity of the colors and the transparency of the brushwork still conspire to give an illusion of

depth. One cannot help feeling, in view of an achievement like this, that Klee, not content to profit by the experience of his contemporaries, had the capacity and the willpower to go back to the sources: to Cézanne. The horizon line stands very high, form is organized geometrically, in a structure so tightly knit as to arrive at a simultaneous projection of the zones of color; add to this the fact that the perspective elements are so disposed that they seem to advance from top to bottom rather than to recede from foreground to background. The perspective is, as a matter of fact, wholly emotional; the effect of optical simultaneity stems from an identity of sensation and conscious-ness—sensation untrammeled by the realistic objectivity of the landscape, and consciousness of his own power, now absolute, to dominate the pictorial medium through which it is possible to establish a fruitful link between visual reality, whose inner meaning the artist discerns, and the "urge to abstraction," the style-forming impulse. Klee, then, seemed to have arrived at a happy synthesis of Worringer's two propositions; but this is the synthesis which, at every period in the history of art, has made possible the creation of masterpieces.

It was from Cubism, logically speaking, that Klee derived the identity of space and time characteristic of his work of 1914 and the next few years. For the time being, it was an identity that took concrete form in the geometrical succession of planes; then, leaving Cubism behind, the notion of "real duration" as postulated by Bergson was entirely segregated from the physical dimensions and became a psychological duration. But it was not by chance that in 1914 Klee painted several pictures directly inspired by Cubism. Such is *Homage to Picasso* (Peter A. Rübel Collection, Cos Cob, Conn.), which is a direct allusion to the Spanish painter, to the Picasso of Analytical Cubism, to his ovals and geometrical decompositions of the constructive elements of objects and figures. But the chromatic richness of

THE NIESEN, 1915. WATERCOLOR.
HERMANN AND MARGUERITE RUPF FOUNDATION, BERN.

Klee's palette and his expressionist background being what
they were, his color could never be reduced beyond a certain
pitch. Space is organized in the cubist manner, contained
within the limits of a many-faceted polygon; yet not only do
his colors remain rich and vibrant, but the pictorial texture
itself assumes a shaping power, a compelling presence. Cubism
enabled Klee to dispense with the descriptive handling of
space; it helped him to work out a more effective pictorial

TEMPLE OF THE SECT OF THE GREEN HORN, 1917. WATERCOLOR.
ELSA SCHMID COLLECTION, RYE, N.Y.

dimension than that of Expressionism had been. This is observable in *Abstraction: Colored Circles with Colored Bands* (Klee Foundation, Bern), also dating to 1914, in which the entire spatial dimension of the composition emerges from the rhythm of contrasting forms—forms which, though once objects, have now become purified geometric elements. It might even be said that by means of Cubism Klee contrived to go beyond not only a certain way of painting, but a whole condition of art.

Yet his nature led him to avoid any set rule too rigidly Cartesian in character; even human reason had to be considered in a critical light, just as the promptings of impulse had to be elaborated critically. Klee therefore stands at an equal distance from Picasso and Delaunay. There is in him a contrast between the "function" of form and the irrationality of impulse which was characteristic of his whole artistic experience, up to the last years of his life; and a fruitful contrast it was, for the will

ABSTRACTION: COLORED CIRCLES WITH COLORED BANDS, 1914.
WATERCOLOR. KLEE FOUNDATION, BERN.

to art, the "Kunstwollen" so deeply rooted in German culture, was in his case strong enough to achieve a synthesis of opposites. But with Klee this "Kunstwollen" never became a will to power; he stood aloof from the Nietzschean conception of the superman and the Dionysiac, aloof too, by nature, from any form of hedonism or irresponsibility. Hence the importance now of the fact that he had been able to overcome those decadent elements which entered into the poetics of Expressionism. His own work he always regarded as being in the nature of a commitment, of an active responsibility toward his fellow men and even toward society at large. His, it is true, was not a deliberate effort to break with the past, such as we find exemplified in Picasso's work; it was, rather, an analytical self-communion accomplished on the strength, not of a will to power, but of a will to participation.

Red and White Domes (Clifford Odets Collection, New York) is another watercolor of 1914 similar in theme to *Before the Gates of Kairouan*. It too is the picture of a town, but one devoid of any concern for the picturesque; the succession of geometric planes on the two-dimensional surface of the paper is more strongly marked, while the illusion of depth and perspective has been abolished altogether. Space is built up entirely in the flat, in terms of surfaces modulated by color; but the sense of reality is maintained, and maintained as an active presence, not as a passive quantity merely observed from the outside, for the artist exerts himself within space and, instead of describing it, identifies himself with it. Indeed, he goes further: the profiles of the domes are made to give structure and strength to the sign; and by virtue of color textures and transparencies which, had they not been merged in a form-color synthesis, might have seemed almost like a concession to realistic lighting effects, the sign is effectively isolated, not as an outline but as a dynamic component—hence a structural element—of the composition. So now, having worked out a composition so compact, and a style so perfectly suited to it, Klee could turn his attention to reconstructing the image, freely and boldly.

The Niesen (Rupf Foundation, Bern) is a watercolor executed in 1915, a year after his return from Tunis, at a time when the war, the death of friends (Macke had already been killed in action) and the dispersion of the art circles in which he moved had profoundly modified the psychology of the painter, and had led him to reconsider man's relations with reality from a more dramatic point of view. Nevertheless Klee continued to draw abundantly—he could not do otherwise—on the wealth of memories and sensations of the previous year. The great blue pyramid here, a concrete element of stability, is like a statement of his faith in the emotive potential of reality. But the colors, even more refined than in his watercolors of 1914, are now autonomous; they serve to break forms up into an arbitrary configuration, but one that answers to the perfect logic of both the formal and emotional organization of the picture. Through the workings of memory the psychological impact gains in intensity and expressive power. The vision of a city is expressed in even more dynamic terms in the *Temple of the Sect of the Green Horn* (1917, Elsa Schmid Collection, Rye, N.Y.), without impairing, however, the fantastic quality of the landscape, in this case accentuated by the very sobriety of the mysterious, deep-toned colors.

After the happy exuberance of his 1914 watercolors, Klee settled now into a subdued key of intimate self-communion, in which psychological values are more tellingly brought out. Confident of his power of reconstructing images out of their apparent structural elements, Klee arranged them, not in any logical order of representation, but in an arbitrary perspective whose pictorial effectiveness, expressive of a reality devoid of naturalism, sprang from the emotional shock it produced.

TREE HOUSE, 1918. WATERCOLOR ON GAUZE.
ART MUSEUM, PASADENA, CALIF.

TOWARD A NEW REALITY

"THE more fearful a place this world is (precisely the case today), the more abstract art becomes, while a happy world produces a realistic-minded art," wrote Klee in his diary early in 1915. [16] To surrender in 1915 to the contemplation of visual reality was out of the question. The pictorial idiom Klee had fashioned, and had carried to so high a degree of perfection and adaptability, enabled him and indeed solicited him now to express the new signification of history. Europe was torn by war. Kandinsky had left Germany and gone back to Russia; Picasso and Delaunay were on the other side of the trenches, no contact with them was possible; Macke had been killed in action in the first weeks of the war, and Franz Marc, one of Klee's closest friends, fell at Verdun in 1916. Klee himself, as a German citizen, was called up in 1916 and, as luck would have it, was assigned to a reserve unit far behind the lines. He felt a keen sense of isolation but went on working hard, alone with his thoughts and his intuitions, intent on expressing a "meaning of the hour" very different now from what it had been at Tunis. The reality of things was not the same; it lay deeper, hidden from view. "Everything transitory is only a simile. What we see is but a suggestion, a possibility, a makeshift. True reality lies invisible underneath." [17]

Having rejected an art of hedonistic contemplation, Klee set himself to fathom and record this invisible reality, approaching it out of the fullness of his own human and artistic experience as distilled in terms of a pictorial language of forms, colors and signs. He sought to open up a new avenue of knowledge, not merely to reproduce something already familiar to nearly everybody; he sought to throw light on the hidden meaning not only of things, but of the complex relationships between these things and man.

In 1917 Klee was stationed at Gersthofen, near Augsburg, on the river Lech, and the landscape there inspired several pictures which, in the spirit of their approach to nature, are very different from his earlier ones. Their dynamism re-echoes the lines of force and rhythmic breaking up of the image which the Futurists used with an eye to intensified expression. But whereas the Futurists merely seized on visible things and subjected them to dynamic rhythms, without making any substantial change in them, Klee replaced reality with a metaphysical dimension, above and beyond the organic structure of the landscape; his was a wholly inner vision, first assimilated by his consciousness, then reflected back again, transformed and autonomous. And from his consciousness welled up the forms of known objects, whose dislocation however stripped them of their determinism and their immanence by freeing them from the rules of narrative logic; they thus assume the value of a psychological presentation.

While still in the army, Klee wrote an essay published in 1920 in the anthology entitled *Schöpferische Konfession (Creative Credo)*. Here he voiced his profound awareness of the meaning of his researches, defining the line of inquiry he was pursuing into the significance of reality in relation to his own artistic experience. "Art does not reproduce the visible, but makes visible. By its very nature graphic art readily and justifiably leads one into abstraction. The spectral, fairy-like shapes of the imagination are brought to light and at the same time expressed with great precision. The purer the artist's graphic work is (in other words, the more he stresses the formal elements on which linear expression is based), the more ill-equipped he is for the realistic rendering of visible things.

"The formal elements of graphic art are: points, and linear, surface and spatial energies. A surface element not composed of sub-units is, for example, the energy produced, with or without modulation, by a blunt pencil. An example of a spatial element might be a cloudy, misty dab made by a full brush dipped in different shades of color." [18]

Klee was alluding here to the incompleteness of objective reproduction. The problem was not so much that of extracting certain elements from reality with a view to a pictorial construction of images as autonomous as possible. It was, rather, that of identifying in the graphic and chromatic means a sense of reality existing beyond appearance; and then of positing the work as an affirmation of a more complete truth, embracing not only the structure of objects but also the perception of them at a deeper level than the merely visual zone. It is the task of the artist to pursue this inquiry, to fulfill this aspiration to unveil a more complex truth; and in his task he is moved by moral intentions. The artist's experience of form enters powerfully into the work of creation, but so does the visual— and even more the human—experience of his own life; and abstraction enters into it at the point where naturalistic imitation no longer suffices to express that complexity of both physical and psychic sensations. To render these, in other words to exteriorize them in a concrete dimension, he has at his command the means of graphic expression: points, lines, planes and space. The process is as follows:

"Suppose we develop this idea, suppose we plot a topographical map and make a little journey into the land of fuller understanding. Breaking away from the dead center (point), we make our first move (line). After a short while, a pause to draw breath (broken line or, after several pauses, articulated line). A backward glance to see how far we have come (countermovement). Weigh the pros and cons of paths in several directions (cluster of lines). A river lies in the way, so we take a boat (wave movement). Upstream there might have been a bridge (series of arches). On the other side we meet a like-minded traveler, also bound for the land of deeper under-standing. At first we are joyfully united (convergence), then gradually differences arise (two lines moving independently). A certain agitation on both sides (expression, dynamism, and psyche of line). We cut across a plowed field (planes criss-crossed by lines), then through dense woods. He loses his way, looks around and even goes through the stock movement of a running dog. I too am beginning to feel some qualms. Another river looms up, shrouded in fog (spatial element). But soon the weather clears. We meet some basket-makers on their way home in their cart (the wheel). One of their children has the funniest curls (spiral movement). Later it gets sultry and night comes on (spatial element). A flash of lightning on the horizon (zigzag line), though the stars are still twinkling overhead (scattered points). Soon we reach our first resting place. Before we fall asleep, much will recur in our memory, for even so short a journey is very eventful.

"Lines of all kinds. Dabs. Dots. Smooth surfaces. Hatched and dotted surfaces. Wave movement. Delayed and articulated movement. Counter-movement. Criss-crossing and interweav-ing. Walls and scaliness. Monody. Polyphony. Line dying away or gaining strength (dynamics).

"The happy, even pace of the first leg of our journey, then the obstacles, the nervous strain! Fear and trembling, the caress of auspicious breezes. Before the storm a swarm of gadflies comes at us! Rage and killing. The good cause is our guide, even through woods and darkness. The streak of light-ning brings to mind that fever-chart. Of a sick child. Long ago.

"I have listed the elements of linear expression which should enter conspicuously into the work of art. This is not to be construed to mean that a work should consist of these elements only. These should yield forms, but without being sacrificed in the process. Remaining themselves unimpaired.

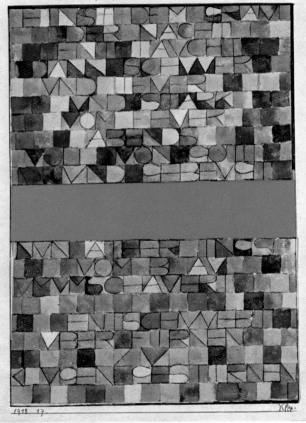

"ONCE EMERGED FROM THE GRAY OF NIGHT...", 1918. WATERCOLOR.
KLEE FOUNDATION, BERN.

VILLA R, 1919. OIL. KUNSTMUSEUM, BASEL.

"As a rule, several elements will have to be combined in order to produce forms or objects, or lesser such. Surfaces out of interrelated lines (e.g. at the sight of fast-moving waters) or space configuration out of energies connected with the third dimension (fish darting in all directions).

"By thus enriching the symphony of forms we increase and vary *ad infinitum* our means of expressing ideas.

"In the beginning is of course the act, but over and above it lies the idea. And inasmuch as infinity has no definite starting point but, like a circle, is without either beginning or end, the idea may be said to have come first. In the beginning was the word, translates Luther." [19]

It might appear that, before establishing the graphic framework of his picture, the artist set himself to find a symbolic equivalent of the elements of reality. But one soon realizes that there is no question here of mere symbolism, for Klee's attention does not dwell on one aspect of reality, a landscape for example, but embraces reality as a whole and filters it through his own mind, through his own mental experience of memory, succession and time. In other words, within a single dimension where time and space are merged into one, he records and fixes a succession of different moments stratified in his consciousness. These he exteriorizes in accordance with an automatic process of formal associations which seems to anticipate Surrealism. With this difference, however: that it rules out the literary element and the over-ambitious description of psychological data. The pictorial realization, however complex, must remain pure in its constituent elements.

Tree House (1918, Art Museum, Pasadena, California) is a watercolor painted on gauze. Its woodland imagery remains fairly close to that of certain landscapes of the previous year, but it differs from them in its chromatic intensity and, above all, in its linework. The motif of the bird is a pure dynamic force rendered in the flat; indeed, the volume of each object is flattened out on the picture surface. Images emerge from an indistinct background, given concrete form, nevertheless, by the thickness of the pictorial texture, by the underlying weave of the gauze, which the artist allows to show through, allows to assert its presence and play its part in the composition. Houses, trees, stars, plant forms, the tiny child at the foot of the ladder in the shadow of the great central tree, the fish-like bird winging its way through the air, all shed their descriptive aspect and elude the meaning normally attached to them. They have turned into other things, other objects, while yet retaining the outward aspect of their original structure.

"Painters used to depict things actually visible on earth, things they liked to look at or would have liked to see. Now that we know how very relative visible things are, we can voice the conviction that, with respect to the cosmos as a whole, the things we actually see are only isolated phenomena and are outnumbered by other, latent realities. So things are expanded and multiplied in their implications, often in seeming contradiction to the rational experience of yesterday." [20] And everything has to be considered simultaneously, for the 20th-century artist does not aspire to an ideal of absolute goodness, and gave up long ago the sterile quest of absolute beauty. "By bringing into play the concepts of good and evil, we place our work within a moral sphere. Evil should be regarded not as an enemy whose triumph puts us to shame, but as a constructive force. A co-agent in the process of generation and development. Ethical stability lies in the co-existence of the primitive masculine (evil, provocative, passionate) and the primitive feminine element (good, fruitful, quiescent). To this state corresponds the simultaneous fusion of forms (movement and counter-movement) or, more simply, of contrasts of objects (coloristically, use of analytical color contrasts, as in Delaunay). Every energy requires a

MESSAGE OF THE SPIRIT OF THE AIR, 1920. WATERCOLOR AND OIL
ON GESSO GROUND. DR MAX FISCHER COLLECTION, STUTTGART.

complementary energy in order to achieve a state of equilibrium
over and above the play of forces. Out of abstract elements of
form, through their unification in concrete entities or in abstract
things like numbers and letters, will finally arise a world of
forms so closely resembling the Creation that a mere breath
will suffice to bring to life the expression of religious feelings
and religion itself." [21]

63

Into the composition of *"Once emerged from the Gray of Night..."* (1918, Klee Foundation, Bern) Klee introduced letters of the alphabet, but his motive in doing so was not the same as that which had prompted the Cubists, a few years earlier, to introduce them into their works. The letter was pressed into service by Klee as a structure, as a compositional element—in a word, as form. It was made to assume, moreover, a semantic value.

"Klee's calligraphic pictures are visual interpretations of texts," Will Grohmann writes in this connection, "just as Hindemith's *Marienlieder (Hymns to the Virgin)* are musical interpretations of poems. The text is conceived anew in the spirit of the pictorial medium. The isolated letter loses the banality of the alphabet and is no more legible than other pictorial ideograms." [22] Ideograms then, not symbols; letters and ciphers perform a pictorial function and may even turn into images, like the large capital letter in *Villa R* (1919, Kunstmuseum, Basel), an element that plays, indeed, an essential role in the intricate vision of the work of art and in that cosmology of which the artist is so living a part, and which embraces both the visible and the invisible worlds. Lost for the painter was the traditional, Christian significance attaching to the contemplation of Creation; by identifying good and evil as two forces equally capable of establishing a moral condition, he went beyond the sense of the Fall and the sense of the Grace that redeemed it. The complexity of his moral obligation called for an action within the very ambit of Creation, and in this participation lies the true purport of ethical values. Thus his *Message of the Spirit of the Air* (1920, Max Fischer Collection, Stuttgart) cannot be taken as an allegory, even though it is more the representation of an idea than of a sensation; this idea, however, which becomes an image, has to be above all else form—in other words, concrete reality. The motifs of this

SCENE FROM A HOFFMANNESQUE TALE, 1921. COLOR LITHOGRAPH.
KLEE FOUNDATION, BERN.

imagery always welled up from the indistinct depths of consciousness: witness his *Scene from a Hoffmannesque Tale* (1921, Klee Foundation, Bern), compounded of mnemonic impulses, memories of things seen and sensed, and inchoate images, which yet assume immediate and very real meaning by virtue of their position on the picture plane and in space—their position, in the picture before us, within a well-organized frame of intersecting lines against a geometrical pattern of colored zones.

It may seem paradoxical, but if these images (and those of other works) were reduced to a naturalistic logical order, they would lose all sense of the real; they would remain in the category of anecdote, even satire perhaps, but their value would be limited to a remembered moment of the past, without attaining any permanence in the stream of time, in the duration of consciousness. The irrational thus regains its validity as a source of inspiration; the laws of chance, to take over the term used by an artist Klee knew well, Hans Arp, imposed themselves as a necessity. Yet, at the time of the creative act, there had to be a coinciding between chance, the irrational sphere of human activity, and the rational consciousness of style. The artist enjoyed the utmost freedom of inspiration, the utmost freedom in the choice of motifs and images, according as they might be dictated by psychic associations of forms; but the pictorial realization inevitably owes much to experience, and this was, and with Klee always remained, his experience of the complex reality of the world.

So though Klee exhibited in 1917 at the Dada Gallery in Zurich, it will be seen from the foregoing that he by no means shared the ideas of that movement, which had come into being as a revolt, under the banner of the irrational, against the "reason" that had plunged Europe into war. Klee's sense of social responsibility made it impossible for him to join an anarchist movement. Participation in the destinies of society, whatever they were—this, as he saw it, was the only salvation. And to participate in the moral and social reconstruction of Europe meant to foster all its aspirations; to transform them, and the logic and instinct behind them, into action; and above all, to communicate them to others. Klee accordingly found himself at home in the Bauhaus and its select company of progressive-minded artists.

INTENSIFICATION OF COLOR FROM THE STATIC TO THE DYNAMIC, 1923. OIL
PRIVATE COLLECTION, BERLIN.

THE BAUHAUS

L ATE in 1920 Klee received a telegram from Walter Gropius inviting him to join the teaching staff of the Bauhaus at Weimar. By January 1921 Klee was at his post, which he held till 1924, when the school shut down. He resumed his teaching classes in 1926 at the new Bauhaus at Dessau, which he left in 1931. These were the years in which the avant-garde movement of European painting, or anyhow a part of it, again joined forces in a united effort to consolidate the conquests of the pictorial language which had been worked out in the years before the war, and to inquire—not only on the esthetic plane, but morally and socially—into the motives behind the creation of that language. Their object in doing so was not to achieve an ideal beauty, or that state of hedonistic contemplation induced by the work of art. The aim of the Bauhaus, as conceived by its moving spirit, the great architect Walter Gropius, was to re-establish contact between the sphere of artistic creation and that of man's social life.

"The Bauhaus of Gropius," writes G. C. Argan, "especially at the outset, may be regarded as a direct consequence and a logical development of Fiedler's theory of art; which indeed, put forward not as a theory of the beautiful, but as a theory of vision, and of a particular vision issuing from the practice of art, found its natural outlet in teaching, in didactics." [23] For Fiedler, from whom Worringer too had taken his lead, "the principle of artistic activity is the production of reality, in so far as through artistic activity reality attains its existence, in other words its concrete form in a definite direction." [24] We have seen how important Klee's investigation of reality was for the determination of forms and the creation of an absolute space-time dimension. His teaching classes at the Bauhaus, and his participation there in a didactical program which aimed at bringing art into line with ethical rather than esthetic ends, came as the logical extension of the researches Klee had already undertaken. "The classical idea of constant, homogeneous space," Argan further writes, defining the didactic spirit of the Bauhaus, "was superseded by the ideal of continuously developing space, of the fourth dimension, of space-time; this was no longer, as in Cubism, a new and revelatory perspective for the contemplation of the world, but the dimension suited to the working out or defining of reality, in other words of the absolute present. This concept of a changeable reality, flowing on with the continuous rhythm of space-time, underlay the formal instruction of the advanced courses; we need only remember how in his lecture notes, going back to the origin of form, Klee explained line as the resultant of a moving point, and surface as the product of a moving line, combining to represent reality not as a definite spatial structure, but as a clashing or interchange of active and passive forces." [25]

Klee brought to the Bauhaus the full benefit of his past experience. And his classes became for him a kind of testing ground for the ideas he had already set down in the *Creative Credo*. The cultural milieu of the Bauhaus was, on the whole, one of constructive rationalism, and Klee, as we have seen, was bent on transposing the impulses of the irrational into a logical frame of reference. But the Bauhaus left him full freedom of action; he was not expected to adhere to any rigid theoretical principles. Nor should it be forgotten that Kandinsky was one of his colleagues. So even though Klee did not take up a position of theoretical rationalism, his cultural surroundings contributed to sharpen his sense of the experimental, and led him naturally to carry out his intention, already clear before 1921, of exploring the physical medium of painting. Klee fully realized the value of pure pictorial means in the work of artistic creation; he was aware of the semantic power of points, lines and space, and

FUGUE IN RED, 1921. WATERCOLOR.
FELIX KLEE COLLECTION, BERN.

their movement on the picture plane; now he set out to test, experimentally, their effectiveness as vehicles of representation and interpretation.

Perspective of a Room with Occupants (1921, Klee Foundation, Bern) comes as a rigorous organization of space in perspective; this, indeed, might even be taken for an exercise in traditional perspective, without any reference to the new space-time dimension. Actually, however, while the perspective is of the illusionistic, descriptive type, the images are positioned in

PERSPECTIVE OF A ROOM WITH OCCUPANTS, 1921. WATERCOLOR AND OIL.
KLEE FOUNDATION, BERN.

accordance with another dimension, abstract in that it represents the invisible, on a plane in which memory acts as an agent of both continuity and will. "Klee's automatism," writes Lionello Venturi, "has been disparaged by orthodox Surrealists as being only partial, because in the arrangement of his images there is an artistic purposefulness which can be rationally justified. But it is precisely from this contrast between Klee's imaginative anarchy and his will to art that his individual quality springs. This quality consists in his intimism, which contrasts with the programmatic character of the work of most of the Surrealists."[26]

In 1925 Klee took part in the great surrealist exhibition held in Paris, but his experience at the Bauhaus, didactic and otherwise, distinguished him from the surrealist painters, and his own esthetic conceptions were very different from those of André Breton. If we examine another painting of 1921, *Fugue in Red* (Felix Klee Collection, Bern), we see that the formal definition of the images is psychological in character: a form emerges, almost like a phantasm of the unconscious, and is joined by other image-forms. But on the picture plane everything is rationally organized, color itself being gradated experimentally, broken down almost to the extent of the solar spectrum. And the rational organization of intuition appears even more clearly in a work of 1923, *Intensification of Color from the Static to the Dynamic* (Private Collection, Berlin), in which Klee seems to avail himself of the two-dimensional projection of geometrical forms on the picture plane, as Mondrian and the adepts of Dutch Neo-Plasticism had done. Klee was undoubtedly acquainted with the theoretical and practical achievements of the De Stijl group, but his own conception of reality was radically different from theirs. He regarded reality as being in continuous movement and thus inseparable from the sensation which, in the particular case of this painting, was a chromatic, indeed an outright musical sensation.

Disconcerting in its novelty, *The Vocal Fabric of the Singer Rosa Silber* (1922, Museum of Modern Art, New York) is a picture that stands apart, unassimilable to any of the tendencies of modern art at that time; it has affinities, however, with the "informal" researches of the second post-war period. The gesso ground gives the watercolor a thick surface and dramatically emphasizes the picture texture; there is a kind of vehemence here, a determination to penetrate and plumb the physical properties of the painter's medium, beyond both geometrical and psychological form, and the printed letters inserted in the painting are not to be taken as symbols or apparitions, nor are they intended to embellish the surface. Klee had achieved complete autonomy in the handling of his pictorial means: the Bauhaus may have taught him the value of the medium in its own right as a vehicle of artistic expression, but taking this raw material he refined it, bent it to the exigencies of his own creative needs, and drained it of every formal notion in order to wield it for its own sake both inside and outside the composition.

This may be regarded as one of the aspects of Klee's naturalism—a naturalism by no means to be confused with contemplation, even less with nature imitation. It was, above all, a kind of intimate dialogue with all things, extending both to those with well-defined forms and to those that are apparently formless. Klee's frame of mind in these years reposed securely on the happy equilibrium of his emotional life, and on the full exercise of his gifts as both artist and teacher. But below the surface there remained a characteristic element of dramatic tension which never quite subsided. In 1923 he wrote a theoretical inquiry into the relationship between man and nature. This essay, entitled *Wege des Naturstudiums (Ways of Studying Nature)*, was published in the series of Bauhaus books. In it he declared that "the artist is man, nature, and part and parcel of nature

THE VOCAL FABRIC OF THE SINGER ROSA SILBER, 1922. GOUACHE AND GESSO
ON CANVAS. COLLECTION, THE MUSEUM OF MODERN ART, NEW YORK.
GIFT OF MR AND MRS STANLEY RESOR.

CAPTIVE PIERROT, 1923. WATERCOLOR AND OIL.
ROBERT H. TANNAHILL COLLECTION, GROSSE POINTE FARMS, MICH.

ACTOR, 1923. OIL.
FELIX KLEE COLLECTION, BERN.

within the realm of nature." [27] While it is the *conditio sine qua non* of all artistic activity, nature is not to be interpreted from a single point of view, that of apparent visual phenomena, for it embraces the whole of the human condition, and therefore also embraces the relationship between being and the world, between *Sein* und *Dasein*. This conception of nature, then, is an ethical one, not a hedonistic one, and from his relationship with nature the artist should gain a new awareness, a new knowledge, and not merely fall back on the standards of the past; to do so would signify "non-being." The image-forms born of different sensations—i.e. produced at different moments of this relationship—may coincide with the natural appearance of things, but need not necessarily do so; and the coincidence, whenever it occurs, always takes place *a posteriori*.

In *View of a Mountain Sanctuary* (1926, Frau Branka Musulin Collection, Bad Homburg) Klee achieved a total expression of nature, not only its outward appearance but also its inner life; this is a cosmic image, embracing past and present and the full complexity of a world in growth. On the other hand, in *Captive Pierrot* (1923, Robert H. Tannahill Collection, Grosse Pointe Farms, Mich.), the image emerges from the unfathomable depths of consciousness and assumes a vaguely human form. Such too, but with greater clarity and felicity of expression, appears the *Actor* (1923, Felix Klee Collection, Bern), and even more so the *Battle Scene from the Comic Operatic Fantasy "The Seafarer"* (1923, Mrs Trix Dürst-Haass Collection, Basel), where the freaks of consciousness, floating on the geometrically patterned surface, emerge from the irrational into the light of reason, which alone can tame and subdue them, or anyhow bend them to its own requirements.

Here, tellingly summed up, was Klee's inimitable way of interpreting nature: his will and his mind strenuously intervene, and indeed every pictured action corresponds to an idea, as

BATTLE SCENE FROM THE COMIC OPERATIC FANTASY "THE SEAFARER", 1923.
WATERCOLOR AND OIL. FRAU TRIX DÜRST-HAASS COLLECTION, MUTTENZ/BASEL.

Klee himself made clear in another of his theoretical essays, the *Pädagogisches Skizzenbuch (Pedagogical Sketchbook)*, published in 1925. "Thought," he wrote, "is the medium between earth and cosmos." [28] Thought also involves awareness of the painter's craft, of his technical means, of the work which in itself is artistic creation, as set forth in the Bauhaus manifesto of 1919: "The artist is a superior craftsman. By the grace of

PASTORALE, 1927. TEMPERA ON CANVAS MOUNTED ON WOOD. MUSEUM OF
MODERN ART, NEW YORK. MRS JOHN D. ROCKEFELLER, JR. FUND AND EXCHANGE.

CHOSEN SITE, 1927. WATERCOLOR AND PEN.
PRIVATE COLLECTION.

heaven, in rare moments of inspiration beyond the control of the will, his handiwork may blossom unawares into art. But proficiency in his craft is essential to every artist. Therein lies the source of all creative work." [29]

In 1924 Klee gave a lecture at Jena in which he attempted to communicate to the public, in the simplest terms, the results and significance of his artistic experience. "Let me use a simile. The artist, you might say, is like a tree. He has managed to cope with this bewildering world pretty well, we shall assume, in his own quiet way. He has found his bearings well enough to set order into the swirl of his impressions and experiences. This orientation among the things of nature and life, this order with all its many ramifications, I liken to the roots of the tree. From these roots comes the sap that streams through the artist and through his eye, for he is the trunk of the tree. Under the pressure of this mighty flow, he infuses what he sees into his work. And just as the foliage spreads out in time and space, visible from all sides, so grows the artist's work." [30]

He then proceeded to emphasize the necessity for close contact with nature, which, by the same token, is also the necessity for human values in the work of art. And he concluded: "I dream at times of a body of work of quite exceptional magnitude spanning the entire realm of the elements, of subject, content and style. This of course will remain a dream, but it is a good thing, now and then, to imagine the possibility of such an achievement, vague as it may seem today. Nothing can be hurried. The work has to grow, up and up, and when the time is ripe, so much the better. We today can only go on with the search. We have found component parts, but not yet the whole. We do not yet have this ultimate force, for 'the people are not with us'. But we are looking for a people, we began the search at the Bauhaus. There we began with a community to which we dedicate everything we have." [31]

Klee by now had given clear definition to his art theories, as is shown both by his writings and his lecture notes at the Bauhaus. But his pictorial researches did not stop there. Everything vital is involved in a process of movement and growth, and the style of each successive picture must to some extent reflect the moment of its birth, must be geared to express a

THE SHIPS DEPART, 1927. OIL.
WERNER ALLENBACH COLLECTION, BERN.

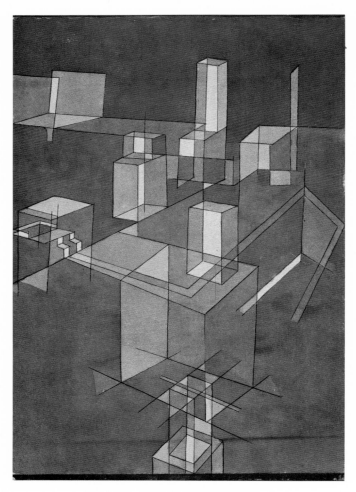

ITALIAN TOWN, 1928. WATERCOLOR.
FELIX KLEE COLLECTION, BERN.

UNCOMPOSED COMPONENTS IN SPACE, 1929. WATERCOLOR AND PEN.
PRIVATE COLLECTION, BELP, SWITZERLAND.

new meaning of the world. The years Klee spent first at Weimar, then at Dessau, were happy and creative years, as an endless variety of motifs sprang from his imagination and took shape in his work. The ideograms of his script pictures of 1918 reappeared, but completely transformed now in such works as *Pastorale* (1927, Museum of Modern Art, New York); here the printed letter has become a pure graphic sign, as the artist made his way back from the alphabet to hieroglyphics, to the archetype of language, to use an expression which Klee had adopted —in a more complex sense, however—in his Jena lecture. Elsewhere, in *Italian Town* (1928, Felix Klee Collection, Bern) and *Uncomposed Components in Space* (1929, Private Collection, Belp, Switzerland), he reverted to the three-dimensional space of 1921, but now the images sought out a geometrical rather than a psychological order. And even familiar images, like *Cat and Bird* (1928, Dr F. H. Hirschland Collection, Harrison, N.Y.), or images of the unconscious transmuted into forms, are arranged in a counterpoint of geometric elements: the square muzzle of the cat, the triangles of the sails in *The Ships Depart* (1927, Allenbach Collection, Bern), the full moon patterned with squares and the houses of an ideal city like *Chosen Site* (1927, Private Collection). And all this without stifling the creative spontaneity of these images, and above all without allowing the compact order of the composition to detract from the chromatic richness whose vital task it is to give life and form to what originally was merely an indistinct sensation, a happy stream of impulse.

The role and significance of color continued to be Klee's chief concern, for color is the most impalpable and mercurial element on which the artist has to bring his esthetic and visual experience continually to bear. Klee's color is abstract because unreal, or better, because transmuted; he felt the need, however, to particularize it in nature, with the result that in

CAT AND BIRD, 1928. OIL ON CANVAS.
DR F. H. HIRSCHLAND COLLECTION, HARRISON, N.Y.

his color all sensations meet and mingle. In 1926 Klee made another trip to Italy in search of "small or big adventures in color." [32] From December 1928 to January 1929 he was in Egypt; the summer of 1929 saw him in the South of France. The light of these places, so very different from one to the other, intensified the solar clarity of his paintings. But it was not only the light that impinged on his senses and stirred his emotions;

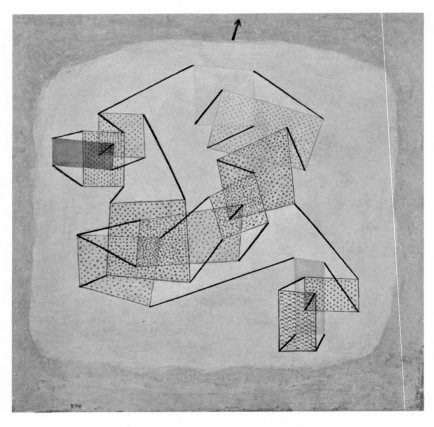

HOVERING (BEFORE THE ASCENT), 1930. OIL.
KLEE FOUNDATION, BERN.

it was also the sense of history that was brought home to him there, especially in Egypt, where he found an age-old civilization which seemed to correspond to his idea of creation, to a logical order of human impulses, to the functional character of the innermost urges ingrained in the human personality. His impressions of these trips, and of this civilization so deeply embedded in the centuries as to seem altogether timeless, were stored up within him and he drew on them for years. *Highway and Byways* (1929, Private Collection, Cologne) is a

GARDEN IN BLOOM, 1930. PASTEL AND SIZE PAINT.
WERNER ALLENBACH COLLECTION, BERN.

HIGHWAY AND BYWAYS, 1929. OIL.
PRIVATE COLLECTION, COLOGNE.

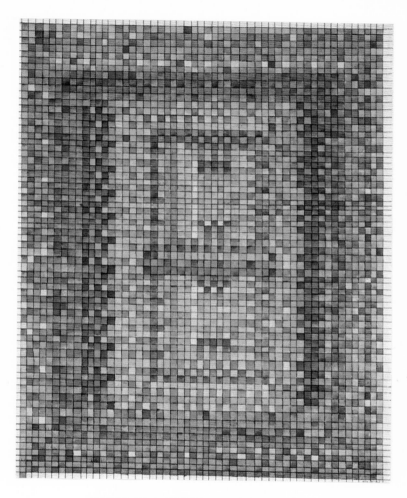

PORTAL OF A MOSQUE, 1931. WATERCOLOR.
RALPH F. COLIN COLLECTION, NEW YORK.

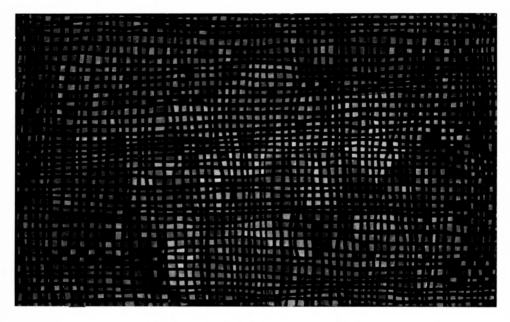

OUTSIDE COLORFUL LIFE, 1931. WATERCOLOR.
PRIVATE COLLECTION, BELP, SWITZERLAND.

network of lines on a plane in deeply receding perspective, which seems to extend to infinity precisely because it eludes the time dimension; the representation of the stone has the value of a hieroglyph. The neo-plastic geometry of *Garden in Bloom* (1930, Allenbach Collection, Bern) is modified, loosened up by color and perhaps even more by the vibrancy with which the artist imbues the color texture. In the same way, the experimentalism of the geometric forms in *Hovering* (1930, Klee Foundation, Bern) is redeemed by the luminous, indistinct space in which those forms loom up. Again, in *Portal of a Mosque* (1931,

CLASSIC COAST, 1931. OIL.
MRS STANLEY R. RESOR COLLECTION, NEW CANAAN, CONN.

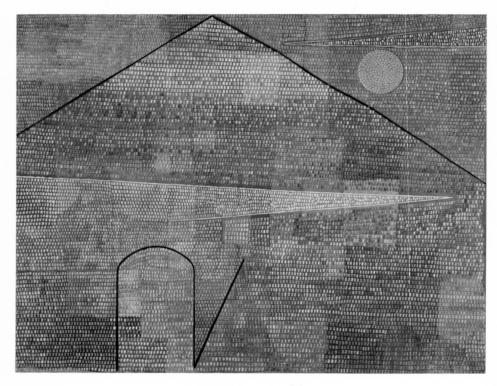

AD PARNASSUM, 1932. OIL.
KUNSTMUSEUM, BERN.

Ralph F. Colin Collection, New York), the concentration of
forms is lightened by a color scheme reminiscent of mosaic work.

Gradually, then, light had become constructive. This was
the period that saw Klee composing pictures in a divisionist
vein: *Outside Colorful Life* (1931, Private Collection, Belp),
Classic Coast (1931, Mrs Stanley R. Resor Collection, New

Canaan, Conn.), *Ad Parnassum* (1932, Kunstmuseum, Bern), and still others. But his was a divisionism which had nothing in common with that of Seurat, and nothing in common either with that of Segantini, a painter whom Klee had admired in his youth. The guide lines of these compositions are strongly marked, and the graphic elements are fitted into a chromatic constellation of dots, thus lending support to the latter in their task of articulating the composition; for the sign too is light and in this non-naturalistic dimension it serves as a means of scansion, as a logical caesura taking the place of the narrative pause and of the spacing of objects in objective representations of landscape. These divisionist pictures seem to come as the concrete aftermath of the rationalistic experiment which Klee carried out, in his own manner, needless to say, within the framework of the Bauhaus. But the Bauhaus was now in disruption, its ideals and its very existence violently threatened by the reactionary forces irresistibly on the rise in Germany, which stigmatized it as an instrument of internationalism. Gropius had withdrawn in 1928; in 1933 the Nazis, having come to power, closed down the Bauhaus. Klee had already left it in 1931 for a professorship at the Düsseldorf Academy. But at Dessau he had finished his task at the Bauhaus and he now felt the need of a fresh start. Storm clouds were gathering over Europe, and Klee foresaw the tragedy ahead. Peace, freedom, and the rediscovery through the work of art of man's social vocation—these were the aims the Bauhaus had set itself and struggled for. In their stead came war, dictatorship and social anarchy. The Nazis branded Klee as a foreigner and accused him of being a Jew. In December 1933 he left Germany for good and settled in Bern. In 1937 seventeen of his works figured in the exhibition of "degenerate art" organized by the Nazis in Munich. For Germany Europe had ceased to exist, except as enemy territory to conquer and despoil.

SCHOLAR, 1933. WATERCOLOR ON PLASTER.
PRIVATE COLLECTION, BELP, SWITZERLAND.

THE SENSE OF DEATH

THE *Mask of Fear* (Dr Allan Roos Collection, New York) is an oil painting of 1932 whose theme seems to anticipate the anguish of mind which tormented Klee in the last years of his life, and which changed the terms of his relationship with the phenomenological world. It is hardly necessary to add that this anguish had nothing to do with the terror felt by a man at the mercy of other men or in the face of the infinite void of death. It sprang, rather, from the realization that European society was heading for disaster, that the artist stood alone and powerless. He saw that this isolation rendered communication impossible; he realized the futility of seeking for "a people" to whom his work might be dedicated. The *Mask of Fear*, then, is the mask of anguish covering the face of Europe, whose myth was again collapsing; it assumes as human an aspect as possible, alluring and monstrous at the same time, a ratiocinative face in a huge oval, sharply partitioned by horizontal lines, and resolutely bent on shattering every obstacle in its way.

In 1932 Klee could still consider this mask with a certain irony, could still subordinate it to his sense of humor. But by 1933 an expression of sadness had come over the human face, as in the *Scholar* (Private Collection, Belp). Two different geometrical values, the oval of the head and the drooping curve of the shoulders, are radically simplified elements but capable in themselves of characterizing the figure typologically. And the figure now is anything but the insouciant portrayal of a happy world; it tells, on the contrary, of uneasiness and troubled consciences. This is even truer of *Fear* (1934, Private Collection, U.S.A.): an organic image, an archetype assimilable to the primordial image of life itself, a unicellular world about to expand and ravage its surroundings like a destructive monster. Man himself becomes an inhuman apparition, nor has nature

Kl. 43

UNTAMED WATERS, 1934. WATERCOLOR AND PEN. PRIVATE COLLECTION, BELP, SWITZERLAND.

the fascination and fullness it had before. We find it twisted and seething in *Untamed Waters* (1934, Private Collection, Belp), reduced to a flat surface and swept away in swift eddies of movement; yet our contact with it remains refreshingly tonic and agreeable thanks to the color scheme of pinks and blues.

Leaving Germany, then, Klee settled in Bern. In 1935 he felt the first symptoms of the disease, sclerodermia, which was to prove fatal five years later. But he went on working as hard as ever and, except for 1936, an unproductive year owing to prolonged illness, his intense output never slackened. He carried on as usual in a spirit of ardent inquiry, never satisfied with past achievements, but always experimenting with new images. Painting with him was neither a game nor a pastime but, before all else, a moral commitment. Death he came to feel in these last years as a lurking presence, never far off, but he accepted it as part of the normal course of things, the destination of the journey through life, inseparable from being and growth,

FEAR, 1934. WATERCOLOR WASH. PRIVATE COLLECTION, U.S.A.

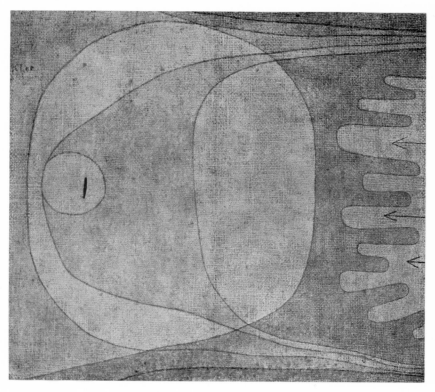

YELLOW SIGNS, 1937. PASTEL. PRIVATE COLLECTION, BELP, SWITZERLAND.

a reality of the cosmos. His inspiration now, needless to say, could no longer be the happy one of light-filled landscapes in the Mediterranean south, of constructive experimentalism pursued with so much ardor in the Bauhaus years. Klee hated war, and war was imminent; Klee needed close and constant contact with nature, and this contact, hitherto serene, was rendered dramatic and tragic by the approach of death, soon to break it off altogether. In a letter to Will Grohmann on January 2, 1940, he wrote: "Naturally I haven't struck the tragic vein merely by accident. Many drawings point that way and say: the time has come." [33]

This occurred above all in the period from 1938 to his death in 1940; till then his painting seldom departed from the imagery peculiar to it. But in the end the change came about, and with it a change of meaning. Now as always the artist sought to combine and interweave all the motifs of his pictorial experience in order to achieve, as he had said in his Jena lecture of 1924, a body of work embracing all these elements and standing as the exact equivalent of life in all its complexity, not only man's life but the life of all things. This in itself was already a dramatic aspiration, and one that had always, even in moments of happy abandon, imbued his work with a far deeper significance than was implied by the apparent whimsy of the theme. "Our beating heart, however, urges us to go deeper, down to bedrock," he wrote in 1924. [34] Ten years and more having passed, Klee felt very much closer to those depths; his painting had become more inward, the motives guiding it lay more and more in the moral sphere of activity. Consequently the works he produced after his return to Switzerland were variously judged, but no one could deny their diversity. A subtle change has come over the space-time unity of the work; modified too is the chromatic intensity, certainly no less great than before, yet less indebted now to the flow of natural instinct.

Yellow Signs (1937, Private Collection, Belp), *Project* (1938, Klee Foundation, Bern) and *Spring Awakening* (1938, Sidney Janis Gallery, New York) are composed of linear elements; but their signs are so arranged as to bring to mind a familiar form, whether landscape, human figure or space. The signs in the first are still supported by a geometric surface pattern, lighter and not so sharply defined as before; they are no longer ideograms or hieroglyphs, but elements of real forms stripped of symbolic allusions and reduced to the bare essence of the image. These

PROJECT, 1938. SIZE. KLEE FOUNDATION, BERN.

SPRING AWAKENING, 1938. OIL.
SIDNEY JANIS GALLERY, NEW YORK.

become even more real in *Project*: man, trees, animals are there, but without any quantitative or even qualitative difference between them. Nor is their arrangement governed by any logical narrative order; everything is subordinated to the rigor of the composition, which is meant to reflect the profusion of growing life. *Spring Awakening* is even more radically simplified: forms and psychological signs are painted on a ground of coarse canvas, whose cross-threads play a definite part in the composition. This picture is a poem, made not of words or sounds but of signs and forms; it has the rhythmical cadence of both poetry and music, to which are added mysterious caesuras and a sonorous profusion of formal elements against an opaque background which brings out their contrasting brilliancy and preciosity. Many are the pictures now in which the artist maintains this felicity of expression: landscapes, ripe fruit, memories of the past float to the surface with a mellow aura clinging to them and awaken sensations which have their justification in the present; more than mere reveries, they come as a kind of pause, a promise of renewal, before the sense of time is lost altogether in a vision of the future and the great beyond.

Stern Visage, *Flowers in Stone* and *La Belle Jardinière*, all of 1939, are like a presage or a warning. The first (Klee Foundation, Bern) might recall Picasso's bony, gangling figure constructions, were it not that the image here is so disturbingly ghostly, even though fitted together from real elements—fragments of a moon altogether lacking in romantic serenity. It assumes a human aspect, vaguely feminine, but quite out of reach, unimaginable except in an order of creation in which the flux of genesis is, as it were, arrested and petrified. *Flowers in Stone* (Rosengart Gallery, Lucerne) also seem to be crystallized in a matter so remote from any direct experience of the present that they acquire the primordial value of things over which time has no hold. *La Belle Jardinière* (Klee Foundation, Bern) again stands for a female figure remote from any effective reality. The artist himself subtitled it "A Biedermeier Ghost." It consists of a simple structure of lines, which here, however, no longer suggest memories, but significantly evoke the presence of that dramatic tension so peculiar to Klee's painting from this time on. Not that this deepening tension, this tragic sense of life, in any way prevented the artist from pressing on with his researches, and from achieving, in the little time left him, still another new stylistic dimension which pointed the way ten years in advance to certain solutions of European painting. *Wood Louse in Enclosure* (1940, Klee Foundation, Bern) is a pattern of interlocking lines which no longer serve either to break down bodies and objects into their dynamic components or to single out the lines of force of the composition, as had been the case in Futurist pictures and often in those of Klee himself; what we have here is the psychological individualization of movement itself, against an indistinct background which the pastel technique renders informal well in advance of its time. An even deeper impression of untrammeled freedom is conveyed by *The Closet* (1940, Felix Klee Collection, Bern), with its plain square of glowing red framed by thick, full-bodied lines. Form is spontaneously generated and does away with every inhibiting limitation, as the pictorial image, thanks to the fluidity of its structure, accentuates the dramatic conflict born of the artist's divided allegiance now to his own heightened sense of being and to the new reality of impending death.

By coming to grips with it and dominating it, the artist removes every semblance and motive of fear: the image of death is thus not confined to the domain of thought, it is not an idea, but is given concrete form in painting. *Death and Fire* (1940, Klee Foundation, Bern) already seems to prefigure the direct vision of death as it was shortly to appear in *Dark Voyage* (1940, Felix Klee Collection, Bern), which is like a journey

STERN VISAGE, 1939. WATERCOLOR AND TEMPERA.
KLEE FOUNDATION, BERN.

beyond the confines of earthly life. "To us," writes Werner Haftmann, "it suggests Charon's boat. More is implied here than is immediately apparent. The significance of the pure signs in this picture is so obvious that they have a far greater power of making us see things than ever a naturalistic painting could have. In the dark rhythm of this pictorial communication it is these signs which transmit the artist's message. We have discovered all this solemnly inscribed within a picture of lapidary simplicity." [35]

It was, indeed, always with the utmost simplicity that Klee re-established contact with reality. He had said that nature was a *conditio sine qua non* of his painting; but death was beyond nature, was even the very opposite of it. But when the artist's mind made itself master of the idea of death, he was able to embody it in concrete, real and yet quite unfrightening terms in a picture like *Death and Fire*. The very texture of the canvas has a chromatic function, even in the white area forming the face of death, and the other colors kindle richly, as if glowing from within. The artist is calm and collected: death is not destruction but fulfillment, access to the ultimate knowledge of life. Thus in his last pictures—and the last is a still life—Klee reverted to a felicitous dislocation of the image and flawlessly fused real and unreal, known and unknown, thereby achieving identity even in the immense variety of his object-forms. The final flowering of his art yielded a new wealth of motifs, as if the artist had found his finest inspiration in the call of death, which reached him more and more clearly now, and to which he was ready to respond. On June 29, 1940, at Muralto, near Locarno, Klee passed away.

LA BELLE JARDINIÈRE, 1939. OIL AND TEMPERA.
KLEE FOUNDATION, BERN.

THE MEANING OF AN EXPERIENCE

Paul klee appears today, two decades after his death, not only as a very great painter, but as one of the key figures of contemporary painting. His work transcends the period in which he produced it, and stands out as a lesson and example to many artists of the younger generation who, in the post-war years, have come to realize its significance and revolutionary scope. Klee's lesson was in many ways more difficult to learn than that of other painters who have also played an influential part in the formation of contemporary taste. It was more difficult precisely because of the complexity of Klee's world, for what Klee carried out in effect was a searching inquiry into the meaning of all things, from the visible to the invisible, above all into the relationships existing between things and the individual, between man and the world of phenomena.

This relationship, as we have seen, resolves itself on a plane of perfect parity, without any one element of the cosmos being subordinated to any other—with all, on the contrary, sharing in creation on an equal footing. Indeed, Klee's work is not only the fruition of new knowledge, it establishes a long-sought-for relationship between the tangible world and society: man himself is both nature and part of a society which, on the one hand, conditions his sensations and, on the other, passively presents itself to the artist, whose action to some extent goes to determine that society. This is not to say that Klee was the creator, before anyone else, of "action painting," such as that which has recently come to the fore in the United States. The elements of his language are much too different, nor was there anything in his make-up comparable to the turn of mind that made possible the dramatic—and, at bottom, still romantic—expressionism of a painter like Jackson Pollock, for example. Nevertheless, the fact remains that certain of Klee's theories

FLOWERS IN STONE, 1939. OIL ON CARDBOARD.
ROSENGART GALLERY, LUCERNE.

had not a little in common with the inquiries into the problematic character of the world made by the American philosopher John Dewey, for whom no separation between being and appearance was possible, and who envisaged art too in terms of human experience: "A conception of fine art that sets out from its connection with discovered qualities of ordinary

WOOD LOUSE IN ENCLOSURE, 1940. PASTEL.
KLEE FOUNDATION, BERN.

THE CLOSET, 1940. SIZE.
FELIX KLEE COLLECTION, BERN.

experience will be able to indicate the factors and forces that favor the normal development of common human activities into matters of artistic value." [36]

Needless to say, the cultural background and theoretical content of Klee's art is wholly European, in the fullest sense of the word. He matured in close contact with the most fruitful developments of European painting, both French and German, in the very years in which a total renewal of the language of artistic expression was increasingly felt to be a matter of urgent necessity. His subsequent activity never lost the significance thereby gained; he made a point of keeping faith with the European spirit, even taking it upon himself to grapple with its contradictions, to enter into the contest between rationalism and irrationalism which broke out not only in painting but, at a given moment, in every field of human activity, artistic, political and social. Klee was not the man to shy away from this painful dilemma; facing it squarely, he sought to resolve the difficulty without breaking the link with the tangible world. Very probably, in the years that followed his death, this approach would no longer have been possible. Artists found themselves constrained by then to opt for one alternative or the other. But Klee held a steady course as long as he lived, never deviating from the moral commitments which, he felt, devolved upon him. If we take for example a painter like Wols, on whom Klee exerted an obvious influence, we can see how he was led step by step to cut himself off from the tangible world, even from memory, in order to go in search of a reality unaffected by variations, not as Mondrian went in search of it, but by isolating it in the irrational sphere of the personality. Klee, on the other hand, sought for reality beyond appearances, but without discarding or rejecting the elements of the tangible world. Reality could only be elicited from within his own experience, his own condition as a man, in terms of a given activity, and the creative process thus came to be increasingly inward, though never quite abandoned to the impulses of the irrational.

"The painting of Klee," writes G. C. Argan, "is prompted by the consideration of man, not in nature, but in society and in a precise historical condition of society." [37] This is true provided we do not limit the term "nature" to its traditional meaning; with Klee we have to interpret it in a broader context, embracing the entire experience of the senses. Klee had written of Kubin: "He ran away from this world because he could no longer face up to it physically. He got stuck halfway, longed for the crystalline, but could not break loose from the mire of appearances." [38] The object of his own search lay beyond appearances, even though he had to go by way of nature in order to reach it. But when nature was also taken to include man—when man, in other words, no longer contemplated it from outside but formed an active part of it—then the problem was not one of reproducing nature by choosing certain apparent elements of it, houses, trees, landscapes and so on, but of rendering its complexity without "getting stuck halfway." For this it was necessary for "the things in nature to be examined from inside," [39] inasmuch as art consists in "the emission of phenomena, the projection of the primary, hyper-dimensional cause, a likeness of generation, presentiment, secrecy," as Klee himself declared in *Exact Experiments in the Field of Art*, [40] which he published in 1928, but which must have been written several years earlier. It is obvious that the artist, being himself a man, being himself generation, cannot overlook society, even if his art, as Argan maintains, stands as an objection to it— objection not in the sense of a refusal, but rather of a critical analysis.

This critical analysis of the elements of the human personality, of nature and society, is also brought to bear on the means of

DEATH AND FIRE, 1940. OIL AND SIZE.
KLEE FOUNDATION, BERN.

pictorial expression. Klee availed himself of the real means at his command; but their reality, in his hands, could not be the familiar reality hitherto associated with forms and signs. He invested forms, lines and colors with an autonomous significance, no longer susceptible of interpretation with reference to the conventional appearances of the visible world. The more so as the projection on to paper or canvas very often took place in accordance with a process of association, along virtually automatic lines, directed and determined at the origin by a psychic impulse. But this interiorization of the creative act did not lead the artist to pure irrationality, first of all because, however subjective, his investigation and interpretation of the phenomenological world was always carried out within the logical sphere of experience. Images of the tangible world, stratified in his consciousness, emerged and took shape in forms, colors and lines, autonomous as we have said, which coincide in a greater or less degree with appearances, but which always individuate reality. This determination of forms results neither in allegory nor symbol, not even when, as in the pictures of 1918, the sign takes the form of letters of the alphabet or figures; the result, on the contrary, is form-content, not form-symbol. Space too—witness the abstract perspective vistas of 1918 and those of an almost cubist order of 1928—is organized metaphysically, over and above every known dimension, both the three traditional ones and that of space-time; it is a psychological space, even though exteriorized in the form of an organic construction.

Always, then, there is this imperious necessity of a logical control of all the elements, conscious and unconscious, that enter into the artist's activity. To interiorize sensory experience, to transform it in the depths of consciousness, to identify physical emotion and psychic emotion, all this was of the utmost importance to Klee; but he knew that none of this was feasible without the intervention of the thinking mind, without concerted action, for both form part of the practical sphere of the human personality. No wonder, then, that Klee so whole-heartedly subscribed to the cultural program of the Bauhaus.

Revealing in this connection is a passage in *Exact Experiments in the Field of Art*: "We want to be exact without remaining one-sided. This is something of a feat, but it need not daunt us. Knowledge, in so far as possible, is precise. The imaginary element is indispensable. What we are after is not form but function. Here too we seek to observe precision: the machine functions pretty well, but life functions better. Life is pro-creation and birth." [41] Life, genesis, creation, the sense of

DARK VOYAGE, 1940. SIZE. FELIX KLEE COLLECTION, BERN.

growth and becoming, and the awareness of the workings of his own being in this evolution—all this conditioned the artist's personality and formed part of his experience. There could be no question of formalism; the mere fact of departing from appearances did not signify withdrawal from or repudiation of the world. "Formalism is form without any function. Today we see around us all kinds of exact forms; our eye, whether we like it or not, feeds on squares, triangles, circles and a host of manufactured forms... The eye feeds on these things and conveys them somewhere to a stomach, which digests them as best it can... As against this we have the living form. The wise man senses the age-old living point, he has a couple of living atoms, has five living, ideal, primary pictorial pigments, and knows now of a small gray spot from which to bring off the leap from chaos to order." [42] And all this in terms of a formation, of a *Gestaltung*—the German word cannot be rendered exactly, for it connotes an experience of form. "The functional motivation of course never stands still, nowhere comes to a stop, and yet even today its limits are laid down, thank heaven perhaps for that. For when it comes to the realm of the secret, analysis breaks down with a blush. But the secret is to pursue one's creative work until the seal of secrecy is broken." [43]

The unconscious, then, is not a negative element; but with Klee it cannot, as it does with the Surrealists, be altogether substituted for experience, which, on the contrary, requires continuous presence of being. The relation with form is thus of an existential character, since form too is a reality, a mode of finding oneself in the world and, above all, in an order which gives meaning to chaos. "Klee is too shrewd," writes Argan, "to have any illusion about being able to represent the unconscious... What he sets out to do is to represent the inconstant but continual pressures... of the unconscious on the conscious, on the knowing mind. The fictitious, conventional coherence of the latter is broken up... Reality, since unquestionably the image is something real and alive, lies neither in the unconscious nor in the thinking mind, but in the continuous attraction of the known and the unknown." [44] The meaning of death too, ever present in his mind from 1935 on, gradually came to be interpreted from an existentialist point of view; he regarded death, that is, not as an abrogation, an opposition to vital activity, to the presence of being, but as an action of which the artist can have no direct experience, an action which, however, represents the attraction of the unknown, open to investigation, and which therefore acquires real value.

All contemporary art, from the beginning of the century on, has resolutely turned away from the contemplation of reality, banished hedonism from the pictorial representation, and set itself to elucidate the hidden facets of man, in all his physical and psychical complexity. It has turned away from appearances, from the reproduction of external phenomena, and set itself to deepen our insight into reality, nature and the cosmos. Of this quest Klee's art represents one of the most authentic and penetrating aspects, not only by virtue of the originality of his pictorial language, which seems to have no more than marginal affinities with that of other European artists, but by virtue of the steadfast moral commitment that pervaded his entire activity, and of his acceptance, though always in a critical light, of all the factors that go to make up contemporary society and culture. The significance of his experience transcends the limitations of time and place; it has its justification in the perennial history of humanity, whose loftiest manifestations it reflects.

TEXT REFERENCES
BIBLIOGRAPHY AND EXHIBITIONS
INDEX OF NAMES AND PLACES
LIST OF COLORPLATES
TABLE OF CONTENTS

TEXT REFERENCES

[1] *Tagebücher von Paul Klee*, June 22, 1902 (DuMont Schauberg, Cologne 1959, p. 132).

[2] Paul Klee, lecture delivered at Jena, January 26, 1924 (published in Jürg Spiller, *Paul Klee. Das bildnerische Denken*, Basel-Stuttgart 1956, p. 95).

[3] Carola Giedion-Welcker, *Paul Klee*, London 1952, pp. 7-8.

[4] From a *curriculum vitae* written by Paul Klee and dated January 7, 1940 (published in Will Grohmann, *Paul Klee*, Stuttgart 1954, p. 11).

[5] Will Grohmann, *op. cit.*, p. 379.

[6] *Tagebücher von Paul Klee*, *op. cit.*, p. 134 (1902).

[7] Arnold Schönberg, *Harmonielehre* (1909-1911), 3rd ed., Vienna 1922, p. 502.

[8] Catalogue of the first exhibition of Der Blaue Reiter, Galerie Thannhauser, Munich 1911.

[9] Wassily Kandinsky, *Über das Geistige in der Kunst*, Chapter V, Piper, Munich 1912 (4th ed., Benteli, Bern 1952, p. 64).

[10] *Idem*, Chapter VI, p. 66.

[11] *Idem*, Chapter VI, p. 66.

[12] Robert Delaunay, *Du Cubisme à l'art abstrait, documents inédits*, edited by Pierre Francastel, Paris 1957, pp. 146-147.

[13] Wilhelm Worringer, *Abstraktion und Einfühlung*, Piper, Munich 1948, pp. 17-18.

[14] *Tagebücher von Paul Klee*, *op. cit.*, p. 301 (April 16, 1914).

[15] *Idem*, p. 292 (April 8, 1914).

[16] *Idem*, p. 318 (1915).

[17] *Idem*, p. 378 (July 1917).

[18] Paul Klee, in *Schöpferische Konfession*, Berlin 1920, Chapter I (see Jürg Spiller, *op. cit.*, p. 76).

[19] *Idem*, Chapters II-III (see Jürg Spiller, *op. cit.*, pp. 76-78).

[20] *Idem*, Chapter V (see Jürg Spiller, *op. cit.*, pp. 78-79).

[21] *Idem*, Chapter V (see Jürg Spiller, *op. cit.*, p. 79).

[22] Will Grohmann, *op. cit.*, p. 144.

[23] Giulio Carlo Argan, *Walter Gropius e la Bauhaus*. 2nd ed., Turin 1957, p. 33.

[24] Conrad Fiedler, *Schriften über Kunst*, edited by H. Konnerth, Vol. II, Munich 1914, p. 154.

[25] Giulio Carlo Argan, *op. cit.*, p. 58.

[26] Lionello Venturi, *La pittura contemporanea*, Milan n.d., p. 41.

[27] Paul Klee, *Wege des Naturstudiums*, in *Staatliches Bauhaus Weimar, 1919-1923*, Weimar-Munich 1923 (see Jürg Spiller, *op. cit.*, p. 63).

[28] Paul Klee, *Pädagogisches Skizzenbuch*, Munich 1925, Bauhausbücher 2 (see Jürg Spiller, *op. cit.*, p. 407).

[29] Walter Gropius, *Manifest des Staatlichen Bauhauses*, Weimar 1919.

[30] Paul Klee, Jena lecture, January 26, 1924 (see Jürg Spiller, *op. cit.*, p. 82).

[31] *Idem* (see Jürg Spiller, *op. cit.*, p. 95).

[32] Paul Klee, letter to his wife, August 1926 (see Will Grohmann, *op. cit.*, p. 72).

[33] Will Grohmann, *op. cit.*, p. 84.

[34] Paul Klee, Jena lecture (see Jürg Spiller, *op. cit.*, p. 93).

[35] Werner Haftmann, *The Mind and the Work of Paul Klee*, London 1954, pp. 196-197.

[36] John Dewey, *Art as Experience*, 4th ed., New York 1934, p. 11.

[37] Giulio Carlo Argan, *Paul Klee*, in *Studi e Note*, Rome 1955, p. 187.

[38] *Tagebücher von Paul Klee*, *op. cit.*, p. 320 (1915).

[39] Paul Klee, *Exakte Versuche im Bereiche der Kunst*, in *Bauhauszeitschrift für Gestaltung*, Vol. II, No. 2-3, Dessau 1928 (see Jürg Spiller, *op. cit.*, p. 59).

[40] *Idem* (see Jürg Spiller, *op. cit.*, p. 59).

[41] *Idem* (see Jürg Spiller, *op. cit.*, p. 59).

[42] *Idem* (see Jürg Spiller, *op. cit.*, p. 60).

[43] *Idem* (see Jürg Spiller, *op. cit.*, p. 60).

[44] Giulio Carlo Argan, *Paul Klee*, in *Studi e Note*, Rome 1955, p. 191.

BIBLIOGRAPHY

The standard work on Paul Klee is that of Will GROHMANN, published in German, English, French and Italian in 1954; it includes a complete bibliography up to 1953, compiled by Hannah MULLER-APPLEBAUM, librarian of the Museum of Modern Art, New York.

Monographs

Paul Klee, Sturm Bilderbücher 3, Berlin 1918. — H. VON WEDDERKOP, *Paul Klee*, Klinkhardt & Biermann (Junge Kunst, 13), Leipzig 1920. — Leopold ZAHN, *Paul Klee : Leben, Werk, Geist*, Kiepenheuer, Potsdam 1920. — Will GROHMANN, *Paul Klee*, Cahiers d'Art, Paris 1929 (including texts by Louis ARAGON, Paul ELUARD, René CREVEL, Jean LURÇAT, Philippe SOUPAULT, Tristan TZARA, Roger VITRAC). — René CREVEL, *Paul Klee*, Gallimard, Paris 1930. — Will GROHMANN, *Paul Klee, Handzeichnungen 1921-1930*, Müller & Kiepenheuer, Potsdam-Berlin 1934 & Bergen 1948 (American edition, Curt Valentin, New York 1944). — Rudolf BERNOULLI, *Mein Weg zu Klee. Randbemerkungen zu einer Ausstellung seines graphischen Werkes in der Eidg. graphischen Sammlung in Zürich, 1940*, Benteli, Bern 1940. — Hans BLOESCH & Georg SCHMIDT, *Paul Klee : Reden zu seinem Todestag, 29. Juni 1940*, Benteli, Bern 1940. — Karl NIERENDORF, *Paul Klee, Paintings, Watercolors, 1913 to 1939*, introduction by J. J. SWEENEY, Oxford University Press, New York 1941. — Bruno ALFIERI, *Paul Klee*, Istituto Tipografico Editoriale, Venice 1942. — James Thrall SOBY, *The Prints of Paul Klee*, Curt Valentin, New York 1945 (2nd edition, Museum of Modern Art, New York 1947). — Georg SCHMIDT, *Ten Reproductions in Facsimile of Paintings by Paul Klee*, Wittenborn, New York 1946 & Holbein Verlag, Basel 1946. — Hans Friedrich GEIST, *Paul Klee*, Hauswedell, Hamburg 1948. — Felix KLEE, *Paul Klee, 22 Zeichnungen*, Eidos Presse, Stuttgart 1948. — Herbert READ, *Klee (1879-1940)*, Faber & Faber, London 1948. — Douglas COOPER, *Paul Klee*, Penguin Books, Harmondsworth, Middlesex, 1949. — Merle ARMITAGE, Clement GREENBERG, Howard DEVREE, Nancy Wilson Ross, J. J. SWEENEY, *Five Essays on Klee*, Duell, Sloan & Pearce, New York 1950. — Gillo DORFLES, *Klee*, Edizioni del Milione, Milan 1950. — Werner HAFTMANN, *Paul Klee : Wege bildnerischen Denkens*, Prestel Verlag, Munich 1950 (English edition, *The Mind and the Work of Paul Klee*, Faber & Faber, London 1954). — Daniel-Henry KAHNWEILER, *Klee*, Braun, Paris 1950 & E. S. Hermann, New York 1950. — Will GROHMANN, *Handzeichnungen Klees*, Insel Verlag, Wiesbaden 1951. — Carola GIEDION-WELCKER, *Paul Klee*, Viking Press, New York 1952 (German edition, Stuttgart 1954). — Pierre COURTHION, *Klee*, Hazan, Paris 1953. — Will GROHMANN, *Paul Klee, aquarelles et dessins*, Berggruen, Paris 1953. — Georg SCHMIDT, *Paul Klee, Engel bringt das Gewünschte*, Woldemar Klein, Baden-Baden 1953. — Leopold ZAHN, *Paul Klee, Im Lande Edelstein*, Woldemar Klein, Baden-

Baden 1953. — A. FORGE, *Paul Klee*, Faber & Faber, London 1954. — Will GROHMANN, *Paul Klee*, Stuttgart-Paris-New York-Florence 1954. — H. K. RÖTHEL, *Paul Klee*, Wiesbaden 1955. — Nilka HULTON, *An Approach to Paul Klee*, Pitman, New York 1956. — Gualtieri di SAN LAZZARO, *Paul Klee*, Paris 1957 & New York 1959. — Will GROHMANN, *Paul Klee*, Unesco Art Series, New York Graphic Society, Greenwich, Conn. 1959. — Will GROHMANN, *Paul Klee, Handzeichnungen*, DuMont Schauberg, Cologne 1959.

General Works

L. SCHEEWE, in THIEME-BECKER, *Allgemeines Lexikon der bildenden Künstler*, Vol. 20, Seemann, Leipzig 1927 et seq. — Ludwig JUSTI, *Von Corinth bis Klee*, Bard, Berlin 1931. — Hermann KLUMPP, *Abstraktion in der Malerei, Kandinsky, Feininger, Klee*, Deutscher Kunstverlag, Berlin 1932. — Willy ROTZLER, *Les Peintres célèbres*, Mazenod, Geneva 1948. — Rainer Maria RILKE, *Lettres françaises à Merline*, Editions du Seuil, Paris 1950. — Maurice RAYNAL, *Modern Painting*, Geneva 1953 (English, French and German editions). — Giulio Carlo ARGAN, *Studi e Note*, Bocca, Rome 1955. — Nello PONENTE, *Saggi e Profili*, De Luca, Rome 1958.

Newspaper and Magazine Articles

Hans BLOESCH, *Ein moderner Graphiker, Paul Klee*, Die Alpen, Bern, January 1912. — Adolf BEHNE, Die Weissen Blätter, Zurich, May 1917. — Theodor DÄUBLER, Das Kunstblatt, Weimar, January 1918. — Theodor DÄUBLER, Das Junge Deutschland, Vol. 2, Berlin 1919. — Waldemar JOLLOS, Das Kunstblatt, Potsdam, August 3, 1919. — Wilhelm MICHEL, Das Graphische Jahrbuch, Darmstadt 1919. — Lisbeth STERN, Sozialistische Monatshefte, No. 52, Berlin 1919. — Eckart VON SYDOW, Münchner Blätter für Dichtung und Graphik, No. 9, Munich 1919. — Hans KAISER, Das hohe Ufer, Vol. 2, Hanover 1920. — Roland SCHACHT, Freie Deutsche Bühne, Berlin, March 28, 1920. — Willi WOLFRADT, *Der Fall Klee*, Freie Deutsche Bühne, Berlin, August 22, 1920. — Leopold ZAHN, Valori Plastici, No. 7-8, Rome 1920. — Helmud KOLLE, *Über Klee, den Spieltrieb und das Bauhaus*, Das Kunstblatt, Potsdam, May 1922. — Will GROHMANN, *Paul Klee 1923-1924*, Der Cicerone, Berlin, August 1924. — Will GROHMANN, *Handzeichnungen von Paul Klee*, Monatshefte für Bücherfreunde und Graphiksammler, No. 5, Leipzig 1925. — Jean CASSOU, Feuilles Libres, Paris, May-June 1928. — Will GROHMANN, Cahiers d'Art, No. 7, Paris 1928. — Jean MILO, Cahiers de Belgique, Vol. 1, Brussels 1928. — Georges MARLIER, Cahiers de Belgique, Brussels, February 2, 1929. — Georges LIMBOUR, Documents, Paris, April 1929. — Karl SCHEFFLER, *Paul Klee: Ausstellung in der Galerie Alfred Flechtheim*, Kunst und Künstler, Berlin, December 1929. — Marc SEIZE, Art d'Aujourd'hui, No. 22, Paris 1929. —

Aloïs J. SCHARDT, *Das Übersinnliche bei Paul Klee*, Museum der Gegenwart, Vol. 1, Berlin 1930. — Roger VITRAC, *A propos des œuvres récentes de Paul Klee*, Cahiers d'Art, No. 5, Paris 1930. — Geoffrey GRIGSON, The Bookman, London, January 1934. — Hans SCHIESS, *Notes sur Klee à propos de son exposition à la Galerie Simon*, Cahiers d'Art, No. 5-8, Paris 1934. — Will GROHMANN, *Klee at Berne*, Axis, London, April 1935. — Will GROHMANN, *Abschied von Klee*, Werk, Winterthur, May 1935. — John A. THWAITES, *Paul Klee and the Object*, Parnassus, New York, November 1937. — *Hommage à Paul Klee*, XXe siècle, Paris, December 1938 (texts by Herbert READ and Pierre COURTHION). — Max BILL, Werk, Winterthur, August 1940. — Ruthven TODD, *Paul Klee, 1879-1940*, Horizon, London, December 1940. — Clement GREENBERG, Partisan Review, New York, May-June 1941. — Aloïs J. SCHARDT, California Art and Architecture, San Francisco, June 1941. — Georgine OERI, *W. K. Wiemken und Paul Klee*, Werk, Winterthur, November 1941. — Jankel ADLER, *Memories of Paul Klee*, Horizon, London, October 1942. — Hans MEYER-BENTELI, *Paul Klee, zu zwei Bildern*, Werk, Winterthur, July 1943. — E. M., *Autour de Paul Klee*, Labyrinthe, Geneva, August 1945. — Robin IRONSIDE, Horizon, London, December 1945. — Stanley William HAYTER, *Apostle of Empathy*, Magazine of Art, Washington, April 1946. — André MASSON, *Eloge de Paul Klee*, Fontaine, Paris, June 1946. — Hans MEYER-BENTELI, *Omaggio à Klee*, Domus, Milan, April 1947. — Max HUGGLER, *Paul Klee. Auszug aus der Ansprache... zur Eröffnung der Ausstellung der Paul Klee Stiftung, 22. November, im Kunstmuseum, Bern*, Kunst und Volk, Zurich, January 1948. — Carola GIEDION-WELCKER, *Bildinhalte und Ausdrucksmittel bei Paul Klee*, Werk, Winterthur, March 1948. — Rodolfo G. BRUHL, *Paul Klee y sus ideas sobre el arte moderno*, Ver y Estimar, Buenos Aires, July 1948. — Giulia VERONESI, Emporium, Bergamo, July-August 1948. — Werner HAFTMANN, *Über das "Humanistische" bei Paul Klee*, Prisma, No. 17, Munich 1948. — W. JÄGGI, *Paul Klee: Wort, Bild, Ton*, Die bunte Maske, December 10, 1948. — Gerhard KADOW, *Paul Klee and Dessau in 1929*, College Art Journal, No. 1, New York 1949. — Jean CASSOU, Architecture d'Aujourd'hui, No. 2, Boulogne-sur-Seine 1949. — Max PULVER, *Erinnerungen an Paul Klee*, Das Kunstwerk, No. 4, Baden-Baden 1949. — H. BEENKEN, *Nachkriegsliteratur über Klee und Picasso*, Zeitschrift für Kunst, No. 1, Leipzig 1950. — M. H. HEINTZ, *Paul Klee zum 70. Geburtstag*, Der Kunsthandel, Heidelberg 1950. — Ruthven TODD, *The Man in the Paul Klee Mask*, Art News, New York, January 1950. — John A. THWAITES, *Blaue Reiter, A Milestone in Europe*, Art Quarterly, No. 1, Detroit 1950. — Attilio PODESTA, *Situazione critica di Klee*, Emporium, Bergamo, February 1950. — *Aspects of the Art of Paul Klee*, Papers by Marcel BREUER and Ben SHAHN read at the Symposium held at the Museum of Modern Art, February 2nd, 1950, Museum of Modern Art Bulletin, No. 4, New York 1950. — Léon DEGAND, Aujourd'hui, Boulogne-sur-Seine, March 1950. — Jacques CHARPIER, *La merveille concrète, Note sur Paul Klee*, Empédocle, Paris,

March-April 1950. — Sonya RUDIKOFF, *Notes on Paul Klee*, Hudson Review, New York, Spring 1950. — Hans Friedrich GEIST, *Paul Klee und die Welt des Kindes*, Werk, Winterthur, July 1950. — Toti SCIALOJA, *Apparizione di Klee*, Letteratura, Florence, September-October 1950. — Hans HILDEBRANDT, *Paul Klees magische Welt*, Wirtschaftszeitung, No. 37, Stuttgart 1950. — H. SCHECK, *Ein Maler des echten Spielens*, Die Kommenden, No. 12, Freiburg-im-Breisgau 1950. — Italo FALDI, Habitat, No. 3, Sao Paulo 1951. — Michelangelo MURARO, *Paul Klee, color y fabula*, Ver y Estimar, Buenos Aires, September 1951. — Gerhard SCHÖN, *Ein Magier kreuzt den Weg. Zu Bildern von Paul Klee*, Rheinischer Merkur, No. 8, Coblenz 1951. — Augusto MORELLO, Commentari, Rome, July-September 1952. — Karl GREBE, *Paul Klee als Musiker*, Tages-Anzeiger, Zurich 17, January 1953. — Gerd HEINNIGER, *Paul Klee et Robert Delaunay*, Quadrum, No. 3, Brussels 1957. — Karl GREBE, *Damals in Weimar, wenn Paul Klee Geige spielte (Erinnerungen an die Bauhaus-Zeit)*, Die Welt, Hamburg, December 12, 1959.

Special Issues of Magazines devoted to Klee

Zeitschrift für Gestaltung, Bauhaus, Dessau, December 1931 (texts by HERTEL, GROHMANN, KANDINSKY). — *Cahiers d'Art*, No. 20-21, Paris 1945-1946 (articles by Christian ZERVOS, Georges DUTHUIT, Pierre MABILLE, Tristan TZARA, Joe BOUSQUET, Georges BATAILLE, Roger VITRAC, Will GROHMANN, Valentine HUGO; poems by René CHAR and Jacques PRÉVERT). — *Du*, Zurich, October 1948 (articles by Arnold KUBLER, Max HUGGLER, Felix KLEE, Rolf BÜRGI, Alexander ZSCHOKKE, Camilla HALTER, Walter UEBERWASSER, René THIESSING, Marguerite FREY-SURBEK, with excerpts from Klee's writings chosen by Carola GIEDION-WELCKER).

Writings by the Artist

Tagebücher von Paul Klee, 1898-1918, edited by Felix KLEE, DuMont Schauberg, Cologne 1957; French translation by Pierre KLOSSOWSKI, *Paul Klee, Journal*, Grasset, Paris 1959. — Various articles in *Die Alpen*, Bern, between November 1911 and December 1912 (on modern art, music, the theater, etc.), including a review of *Die Ausstellung des Modernen Bundes im Kunsthaus Zürich*, No. 12, 1912, pp. 696-704. — Translation of Robert Delaunay's essay *Sur la Lumière (Über das Licht)*, in *Der Sturm*, Berlin, January 1913. — *Die Schöpferische Konfession*, pp. 28-40 (Tribüne der Kunst und Zeit 13), E. Reiss, Berlin 1920. — Reply to an inquiry held among artists: *Über den Wert der Kritik*, in *Der Ararat*, Munich 1921. — *Wege des Naturstudiums*, in *Staatliches Bauhaus in Weimar, 1919-1923*, Weimar-Munich 1923, pp. 24-25 (reprinted in the catalogue of the Klee exhibition at the Haus der Kunst, Munich 1950, and Galerie Buchheim-Militon,

Frankfort 1950). — *Pädagogisches Skizzenbuch* (Bauhausbücher 2), Langen, Munich 1925 (English translations, *Pedagogical Sketchbook*, Nierendorf Gallery, New York 1944, and *Paul Klee : Pedagogical Sketchbook*, translated and introduced by S. MOHOLY-NAGY, Praeger, New York 1953). — Article on Kandinsky, in *Katalog der Jubiläumausstellung zum 60. Geburtstage von W. Kandinsky*, Galerie Arnold, Dresden 1926. — Article on Emil Nolde in *Festschrift für Emil Nolde anlässlich seines 60. Geburtstages*, Neue Kunst, Fides, Dresden 1927. — *Exakte Versuche im Bereiche der Kunst*, in Bauhaus-Zeitschrift für Gestaltung, Dessau 1928, No. 2-3. — *Aussprüche und Aphorismen* (aus dem Kollegienheft einer Schülerin — Petra Petitpierre — an der Staatlichen Kunstakademie Düsseldorf), in *Die Tat*, No. 274, Zurich 1940. — *Über die moderne Kunst*, Benteli, Bern 1945 (compiled from Klee's Jena lecture of 1924; English translation by Douglas COOPER, *On Modern Art*, introduction by Herbert READ, Faber & Faber, London 1947; fragments translated into Spanish with a note by Mathias GOERITZ, in *Cobalto*, Barcelona 1949, No. 2). — Eight poems in *Poètes à l'écart*, by Carola GIEDION-WELCKER, Benteli, Bern, 1946, pp. 105-110. — *Dokumente und Bilder aus den Jahren 1896-1930*, vol. 1 (various writings, extracts from letters and diary, edited by the Klee-Gesellschaft, Bern), Benteli, Bern 1949. — *Paul Klee, Das Bildnerische Denken*, edited by Jürg SPILLER, Benno Schwabe, Basel-Stuttgart 1956 (containing Klee's contribution to *Die Schöpferische Konfession*, his Jena lecture, the lecture notes of his courses at the Bauhaus, etc.); English edition, *Paul Klee, The Thinking Eye*, New York 1961. — *Im Zwischenreich*, watercolors and drawings by Klee, with the text from *Die Schöpferische Konfession*, commentaries by Carola GIEDION-WELCKER, Will GROHMANN, Werner SCHMALENBACH, Georg SCHMIDT, introduction by Werner HAFTMANN, DuMont Schauberg, Cologne 1957; English edition, *The Inward Vision, Watercolors, Drawings, Writings*, New York and London 1958. — *Dokumente und Bilder, 1930-1940*, vol. 2, Bern 1960. — *The Diaries of Paul Klee, 1898-1918*, ed. by Felix KLEE, Berkeley 1964.

Bibliographical Supplement

W. GROHMANN, *Paul Klee, Drawings*, New York and London 1960. — F. KLEE, *Paul Klee : Leben und Werk in Dokumenten*, Zurich 1960; *Paul Klee, His Life and Work in Documents*, New York 1962. — M. HUGGLER, *Paul Klee, Paintings and Drawings*, Bern 1961. — E. W. KORNFELD, *Verzeichnis des graphischen Werkes von Paul Klee*, Bern 1963. — C. ROY, *Paul Klee, Aux sources de la peinture*, Paris 1963. — W. HOFMANN, *Klee, Traumlandschaft mit Mond*, Frankfurt 1964. — W. UEBERWASSER, *Klee : The Later Work*, Basel 1965. — M. HUGGLER, *Paul Klee, Drawings*, Alhambra, Calif. 1965. — W. GROHMANN, *Paul Klee*, New York and London 1967.

CHIEF EXHIBITIONS

Group Exhibitions:

1906, 1908, Munich, Secession. — 1908, Zurich, "Die Walze" Group (traveling exhibition). — 1912, Munich, Second Exhibition of Der Blaue Reiter. — 1912, Cologne, Sonderbund. — 1912, Zurich, Der Moderne Bund. — 1913, Berlin, Erster Deutscher Herbstsalon (22 items). — 1938, New York, Museum of Modern Art, *The Bauhaus*. — 1948, Venice, 24th Biennale (18 items, introduction by Max HUGGLER). — 1949, Munich, Haus der Kunst, *Der Blaue Reiter* (50 items, catalogue containing quotations from Klee's Diary). — 1950, Munich, Haus der Kunst, *Die Maler am Bauhaus* (59 items, catalogue with texts by Walter GROPIUS, Helene NONNE-SCHMIDT, Ludwig GROTE, KLEE, *Wege des Naturstudiums*, etc.). — 1950, Venice, 25th Biennale, *Il Cavaliere azzurro* (17 items). — 1958, Munich, Haus der Kunst, *München 1869-1958* (12 items). — 1958, Brussels, World's Fair, *Cinquante ans d'art moderne* (9 items). — 1959, Kassel, *Documenta* (13 items).

One-Man Shows:

1910, Zurich, Kunsthaus, Bern and Basel (55 items). — 1911, 1923, Munich, Galerie Thannhauser. — 1913, 1916, 1919, Berlin, Galerie Der Sturm. — 1917, Zurich, Galerie Dada. — 1919, Frankfort, Zinglers Kabinett (35 items, catalogue with text by T. DÄUBLER). — 1919, Hanover, Kestner-Gesellschaft (122 items, catalogue with introduction by Paul Erich KÜPPERS). — 1920, Düsseldorf, Galerie Flechtheim (introduction by T. DÄUBLER). — 1920, Munich, Galerie Goltz (356 items, catalogue published in *Der Ararat*, Munich, with biographical and critical essay). — 1921, Munich, New Secession. — 1921, Hanover, Galerie von Garvens (catalogue with excerpts from Klee's Diary and a text by HAUSENSTEIN, *Kairuan*). — 1924, 1926, 1929, Dresden, Galerie Fides. — 1924, New York, Société Anonyme (26 paintings, first American exhibition). — 1925, Munich, Galerie Goltz, *Retrospective Exhibition 1920-1925* (214 items). — 1925, Paris, Galerie Vavin Raspail, *39 Watercolors by Paul Klee* (poem by Paul ELUARD, introduction by ARAGON). — 1927, Düsseldorf, Galerie Flechtheim (50 items, preface by A. FLECHTHEIM and a text by René CREVEL). — 1929, Paris, Galerie Bernheim (40 items, introduction by René CREVEL). — 1929, Dresden, Galerie Fides (150 items, catalogue by Rudolf PROBST). — 1929, 1930 (160 items, introduction by ARAGON), 1931, Berlin, Galerie Flechtheim. — 1930, Berlin, Nationalgalerie. — 1930, New York, Museum of Modern Art (63 items, catalogue by Alfred H. BARR). — 1931, Düsseldorf, Kunstverein für die Rheinlande und Westphalen (252 items, introduction by Will GROHMANN). — 1931, Hanover, Kestner-Gesellschaft (introduction by René CREVEL). — 1935, New York, Contemporary Art Circle, *Paul Klee at Neumann's* (note by J. B. NEUMANN). — April and November 1938, 1940 (100 items, catalogue with texts by J. J. SWEENEY and J. and L. FEININGER), April and October

1948, May 1950 (catalogue with excerpts from Klee's Diary), 1951, 1953 (catalogue with excerpts from Klee's Diary), New York, Buchholz Gallery (Curt VALENTIN). — 1938 (62 items, introduction by Perry RATHBONE), 1940, February 1941 (42 items, introduction by Clark MILLS), 1942, 1945, 1947, New York, Nierendorf Galleries. — 1940, Bern, Kunsthalle, *Memorial Exhibition* (233 items, introduction by H. MEYER-BENTELI). — 1940, Zurich, Kunsthaus (213 items, introduction by W. WARTMANN). — 1941, Chicago, Art Club, *Memorial Exhibition* (83 items, essay by J. J. SWEENEY). — 1941, London, Leicester Galleries, *Paintings and Watercolors* (introduction by Herbert READ). — 1941, Basel, Kunsthalle. — 1941, San Francisco, Museum of Art, *Memorial Exhibition* (introduction by Grace MORLEY, excerpts from Klee's letters); same exhibition held in Los Angeles. — 1941, New York, Museum of Modern Art (texts by Alfred H. BARR, J. J. SWEENEY, J. and L. FEININGER); same exhibition held at Northampton, Mass., Chicago, Portland, Los Angeles, St. Louis, Wellesley, Mass. — 1942, Washington, Phillips Memorial Gallery, *Memorial Exhibition* (30 items, introduction by Duncan PHILLIPS). — 1945, 1948, Lucerne, Galerie Rosengart, *Paul Klee zum Gedächtnis* (45 items, introduction by Georg SCHMIDT). — 1945, London, National Gallery (137 items, preface by Rolf BÜRGI). — 1946, Denver, Art Museum, *A New Way to Paul Klee* (69 items, text by Otto Karl BACH). — 1947, Bern, Kunstmuseum, *Ausstellung der Paul Klee-Stiftung* (365 items); same exhibition held in 1948 in Paris, Musée National d'Art Moderne, introduction by Henri HOPPENOT; Brussels, Palais des Beaux-Arts, preface by G. LIMBOUR; Amsterdam, Stedelijk Museum; Zurich, Kunsthaus, introduction by W. WARTMANN; Basel, Kunsthalle, catalogue and text by Georg SCHMIDT, *Das Grundmotiv in der Kunst Paul Klees.* — 1948, Munich, Galerie Otto Stangl (40 items, introduction by Felix KLEE). — 1948, Düsseldorf, Hetjens-Museum, *Späte Werke* (30 items lent by the Klee-Gesellschaft; articles by Gerhard KADOW, Ernst WILLEMSEN, Günter GROTE); same exhibition held in 1949 at Freiburg-in-Breisgau, Kunstverein, catalogue with excerpts from KLEE, *Über die moderne Kunst.* — 1949, New York, Museum of Modern Art, *Paintings, Drawings and Prints from the Klee Foundation, Bern, with Additions from American Collections* (introduction by J. T. SOBY); same exhibition held in Portland, Detroit, St. Louis, Washington, Cincinnati. — 1950, Basel, Kunstmuseum, *Paul Klee, Ausstellung aus Schweizer Privatsammlungen zum 10. Todestag, 29. Juni 1950* (102 items, introduction and text by Georg SCHMIDT). — 1950, Frankfort, Galerie Buchheim-Militon (36 paintings, watercolors, drawings and lithographs; catalogue by Will GROHMANN with a text by Walter GROPIUS and KLEE's *Wege des Naturstudiums*). — 1951, Palm Beach, Society of the Four Arts (76 items, including 16 paintings from the Schang Collection; introduction by F. C. SCHANG). — 1952, Hanover, Kestner-Gesellschaft (88 items, introduction by A. HENTZEN). — 1952, 1953 (introduction by Will GROHMANN), Paris, Galerie Berggruen. — 1953, London, Institute of Contemporary Arts (50 drawings from the Curt Valentin Collection, introduction by Will GROHMANN); same exhibition held in Hanover, Berlin and Dublin. — 1954, Hanover, Kestner-Gesellschaft, *Paul Klee, Max Beckmann* (catalogue by A. HENTZEN). — 1954, La Sarraz-Lausanne (60 items, texts by André TANNER, René BERGER, etc.). — 1954, Munich, Haus der Kunst, *Klee and Kandinsky*. — 1955, St. Gall, Kunstverein (catalogue with texts by Dr. E. NAEGELI, R. HANHART, H. GEIST, and excerpts from writings by Georg SCHMIDT, Will GROHMANN, C. GIEDION-WELCKER and W. HAFTMANN). — 1956, Bern, Kunstmuseum (756 items, catalogue with introduction by Max HUGGLER; the most extensive exhibition so far devoted to Klee, organized by the Paul Klee Stiftung, Bern). — 1957, Amsterdam, Stedelijk Museum. — March 1959, Paris, Galerie Berggruen, *Klee et Kandinsky, Une confrontation* (texts by Pierre VOLBOUDT, Kenneth LINDSAY, KANDINSKY on Klee, and KLEE on Kandinsky). — 1960, Düsseldorf, Schloss Jägernhof (88 works). — 1960, Grenoble, Musée des Beaux-Arts (120 works). — 1961, Tokyo, Museum. — Basel, Galerie Beyeler (2 exhibitions). — 1963, Amsterdam, Stedelijk Museum. — 1964, Baden-Baden, Kunsthalle, Early Work (213 items). — 1965, Basel, Galerie Beyeler, Late Work (65 items). — 1966, London, Marlborough Gallery (56 works). — 1966, Tel-Aviv, Museum. — 1967, New York, Solomon R. Guggenheim Museum, Retrospective. — 1967, Basel, Kunsthalle (222 works). — 1967, Marseilles, Musée Cantini (184 works). — Nagoya, Aichi Museum (191 works). — 1969, Essen, Folkwang Museum (166 watercolors and drawings). — 1969-1970, Paris, Musée national d'Art Moderne (199 works).

INDEX OF NAMES AND PLACES

LIST OF COLORPLATES

CONTENTS

THIS VOLUME OF THE SERIES "THE TASTE OF OUR TIME"
WAS PRODUCED BY THE TECHNICAL STAFF OF EDITIONS
D'ART ALBERT SKIRA. FINISHED THE TENTH DAY OF
FEBRUARY NINETEEN HUNDRED AND SEVENTY-TWO.

TEXT AND ILLUSTRATIONS PRINTED BY

COLOR STUDIOS
AT IMPRIMERIES RÉUNIES S.A., LAUSANNE
AND PRESSES CENTRALES S.A., LAUSANNE

PLATES ENGRAVED BY GUEZELLE & RENOUARD, PARIS

PHOTOGRAPHS BY

Louis Frohman, New York (pages 3, 30, 50, 75, 76, 80, 87, 91, 93, 99), **Hans Hinz,**
Basel (pages 14, 20, 25, 26, 33, 34, 37, 40, 44, 51, 59, 63, 65, 68, 71, 72, 77, 79,
81, 83, 84, 85, 88, 89, 90, 94, 96, 98, 100, 102, 106, 108, 110, 111, 115, 117),
Master Photographers, New York (page 46), Harry Baskerville, Santa Barbara
(Calif.) (page 47) and Henry B. Beville, Washington (pages 54, 103). Other
photographs obligingly lent by the magazine Du, *Zurich (pages 49, 92, 112).*

PRINTED IN SWITZERLAND